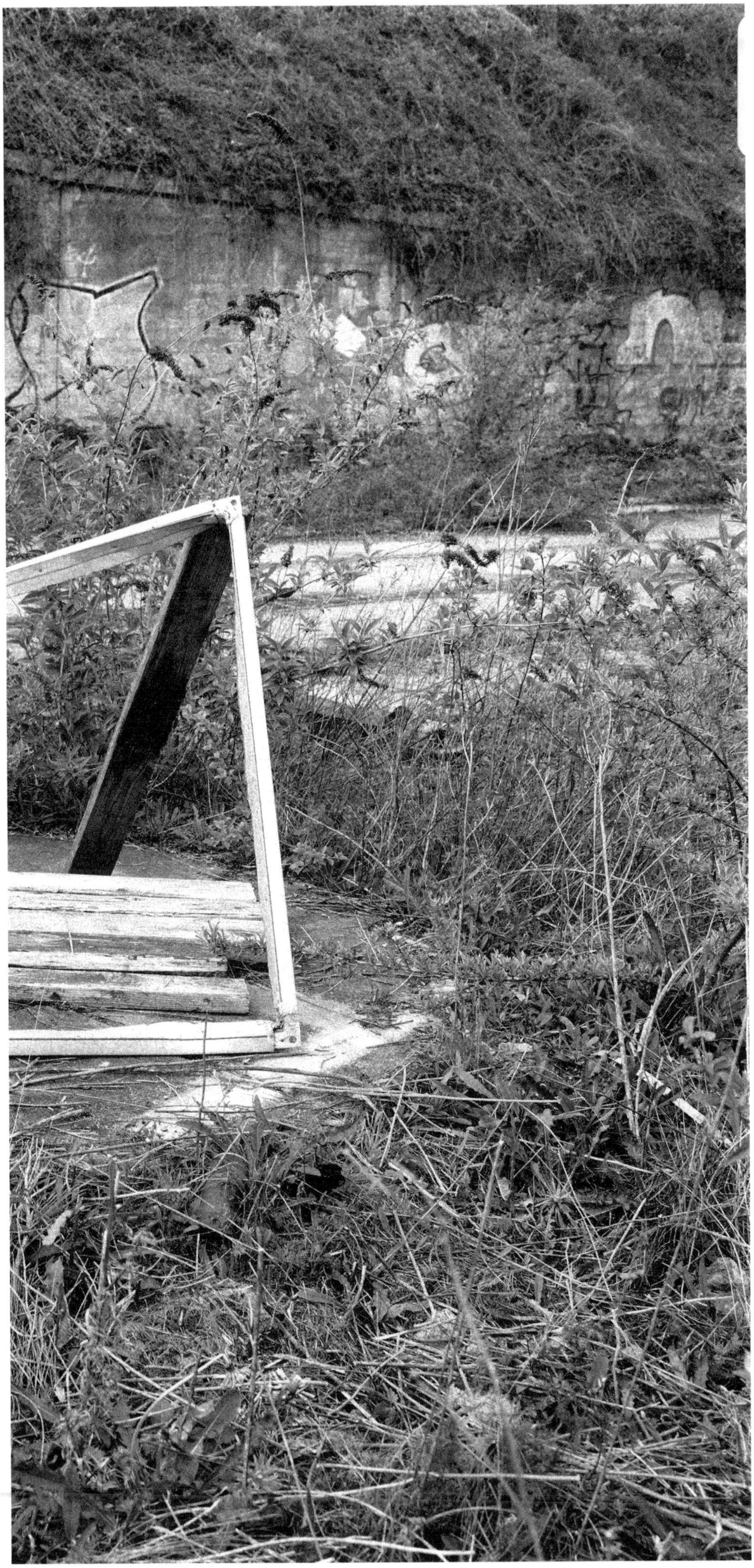

AF600802

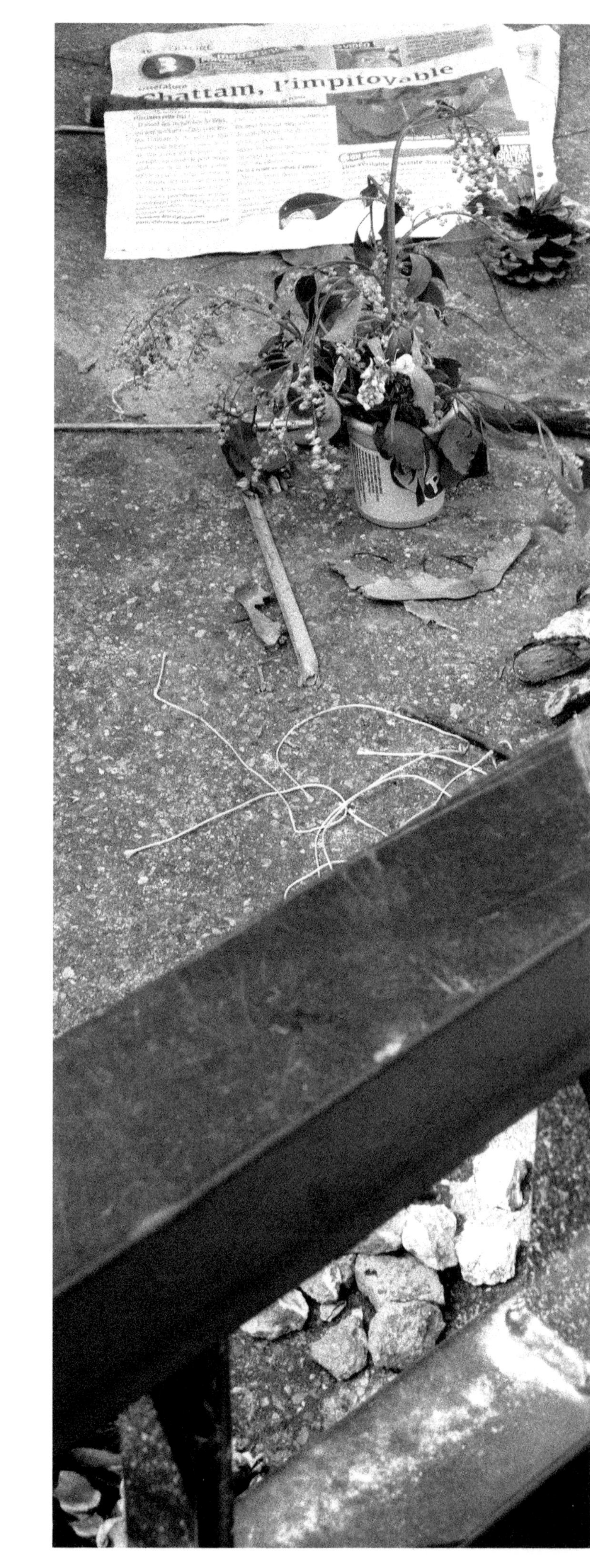
Chattam, l'impitoyable

WANDERING OFF

09m.15s. (Bozar),
Primary Stages series, 2012

La poétique de l'Espace,
Memento series, 2013

Á la recherche du temps perdu,
Memento series, 2013

04m.40s.,
Public Sculptures series, 2012

05m.25s.,
Public Sculptures series, 2012

Djadja,
Memento series, 2013

Ela falava do silêncio,
Memento series, 2013

Le rendez-vous,
Memento series, 2013

Por falar em escadas,
Memento series, 2013

Former un vœu,
Memento series, 2013

07m.10s. (le grand palais),
Primary Stages series, 2013

Do outro lado do rio,
Memento series, 2013

Des toits sous le pont,
Memento series, 2013

O pescador ilegal,
Memento series, 2013

Laisser le temps passer,
Memento series, 2013

03m. 40s.,
Public Sculptures series, 2012

Des petits indiens,
Memento series, 2013

13m.10s. (Extra City),
Primary Stages series, 2012

Wasted time (a sedimental walk),
Public Sculptures series, 2012

08m. 30s. (a sedimental walk),
Public Sculptures series, 2012

07m. 50s. (a sedimental walk),
Public Sulptures series, 2012

06m. 20s. (a sedimental walk),
Public Sculptures series, 2012

12m.25s. (LuFo A),
Primary Stages series, 2012

05m.25s. (booth camp),
Primary Stages series, 2012

08m.40s. (booth camp),
Primary Stages series, 2012

20m.15s. (booth camp),
Primary Stages series, 2012

01m. 00s.,
Public Sculptures series, 2012

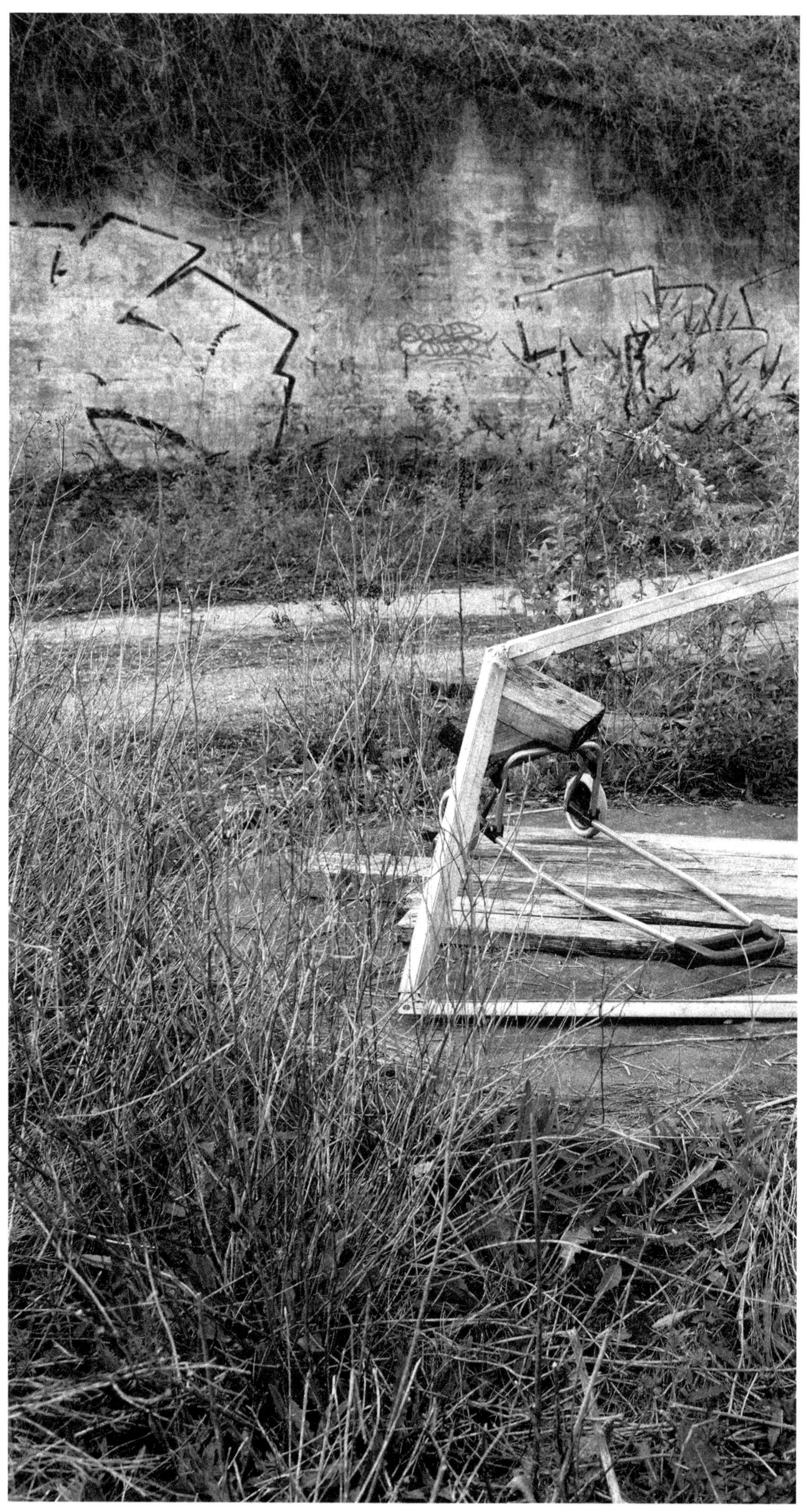

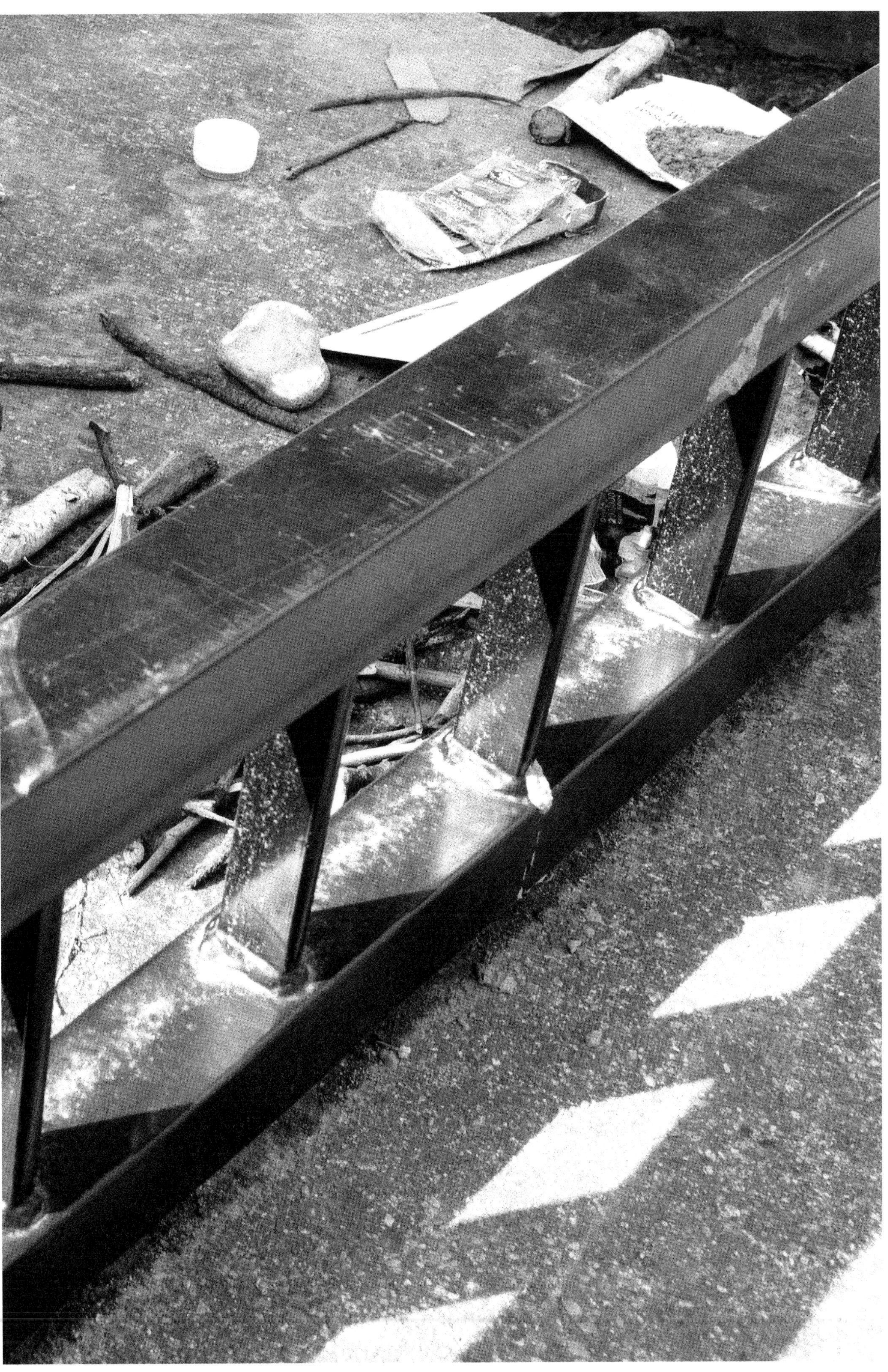

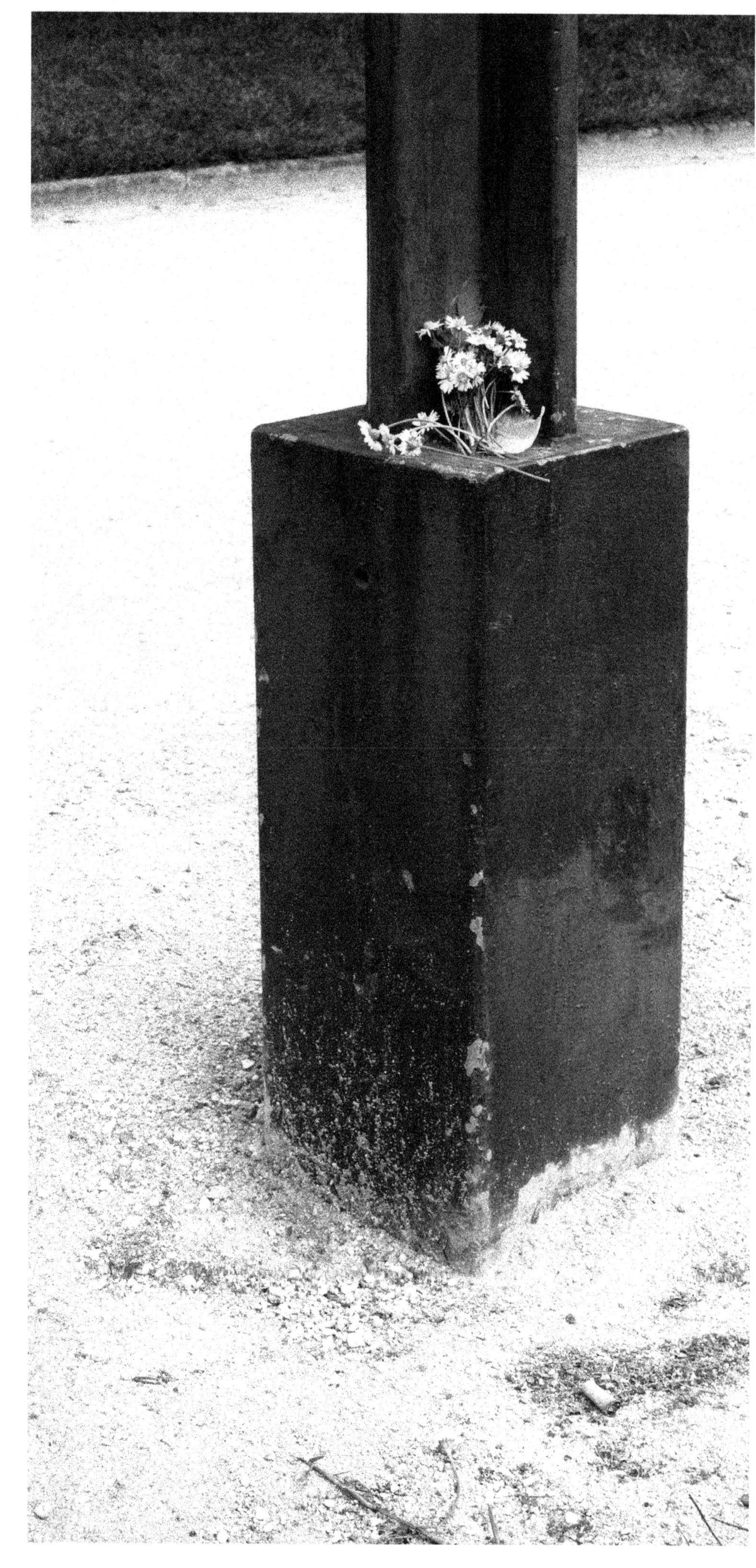

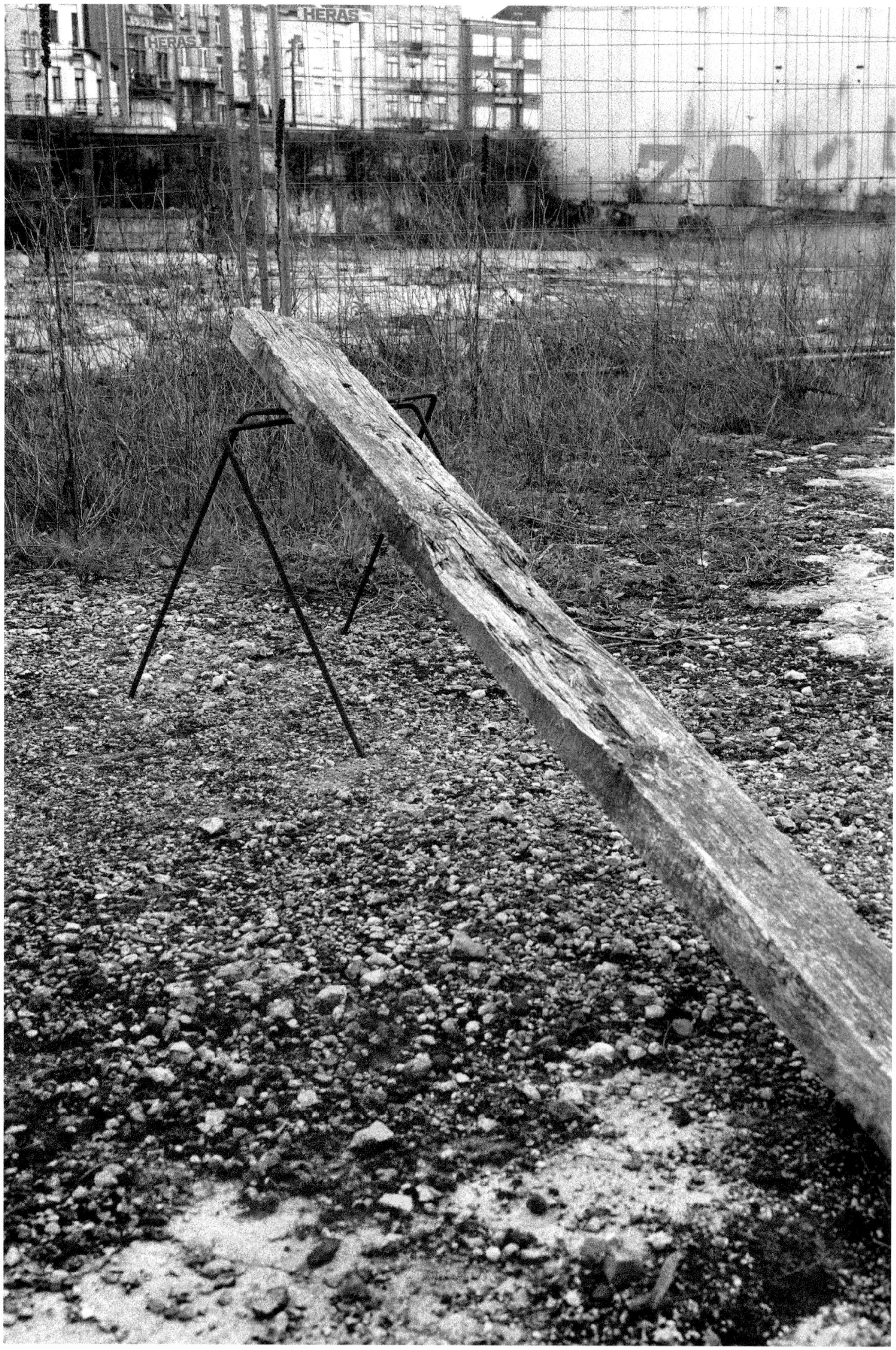
HERAS
HERAS

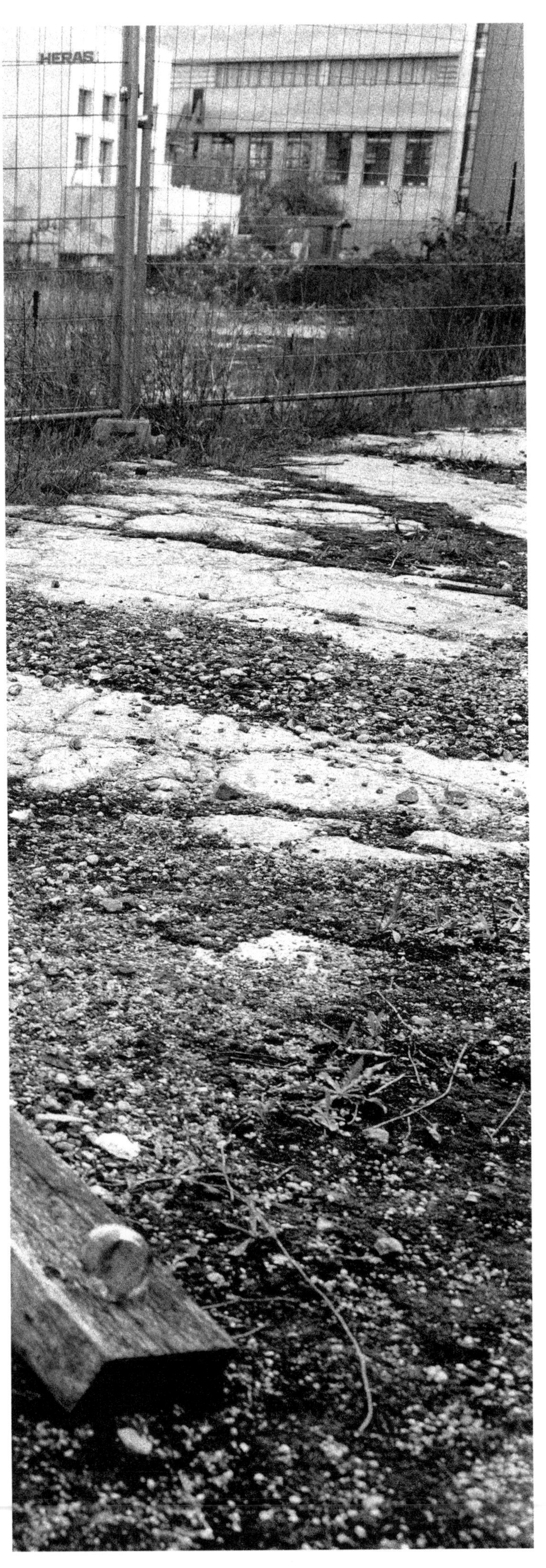
HERAS

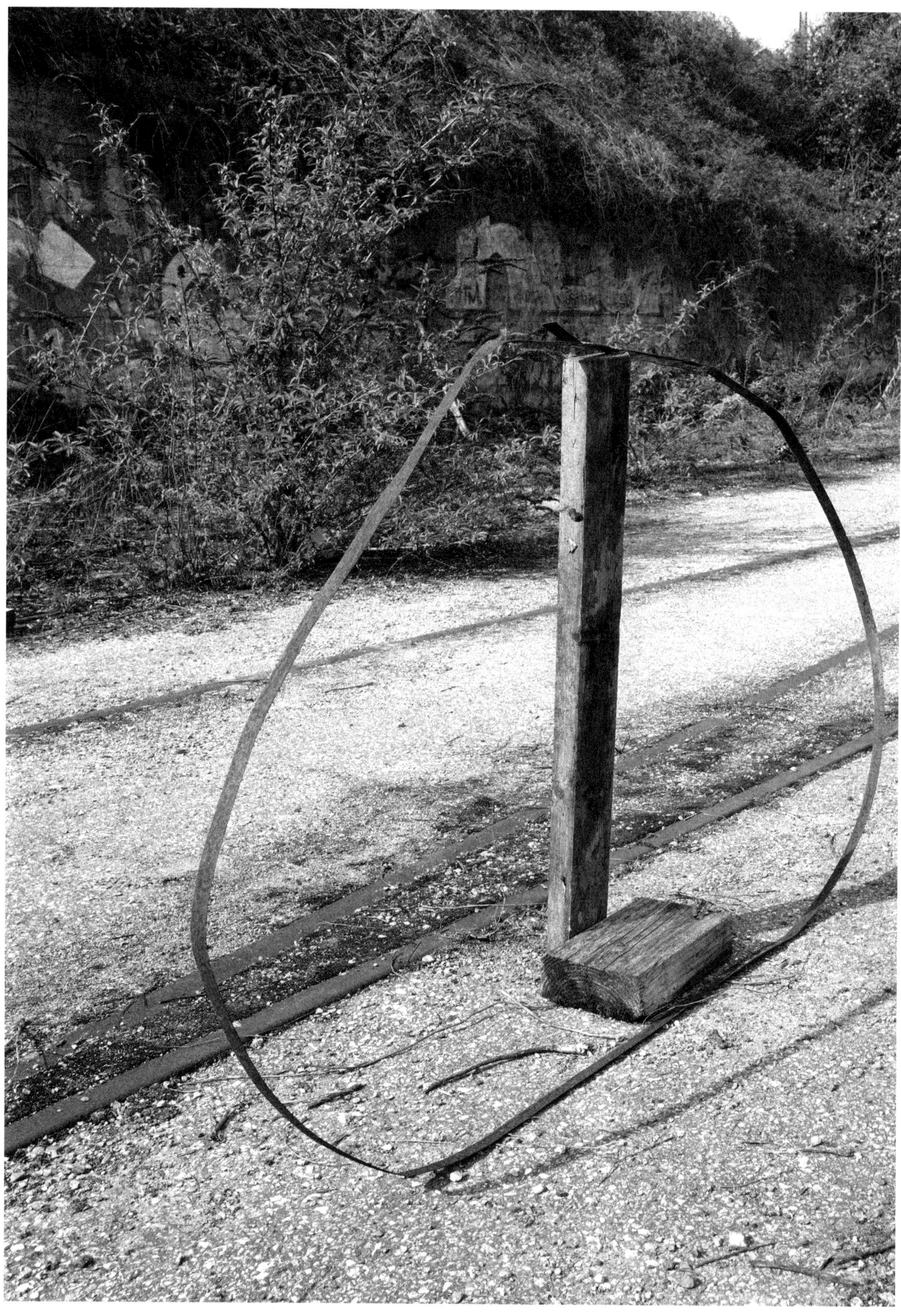

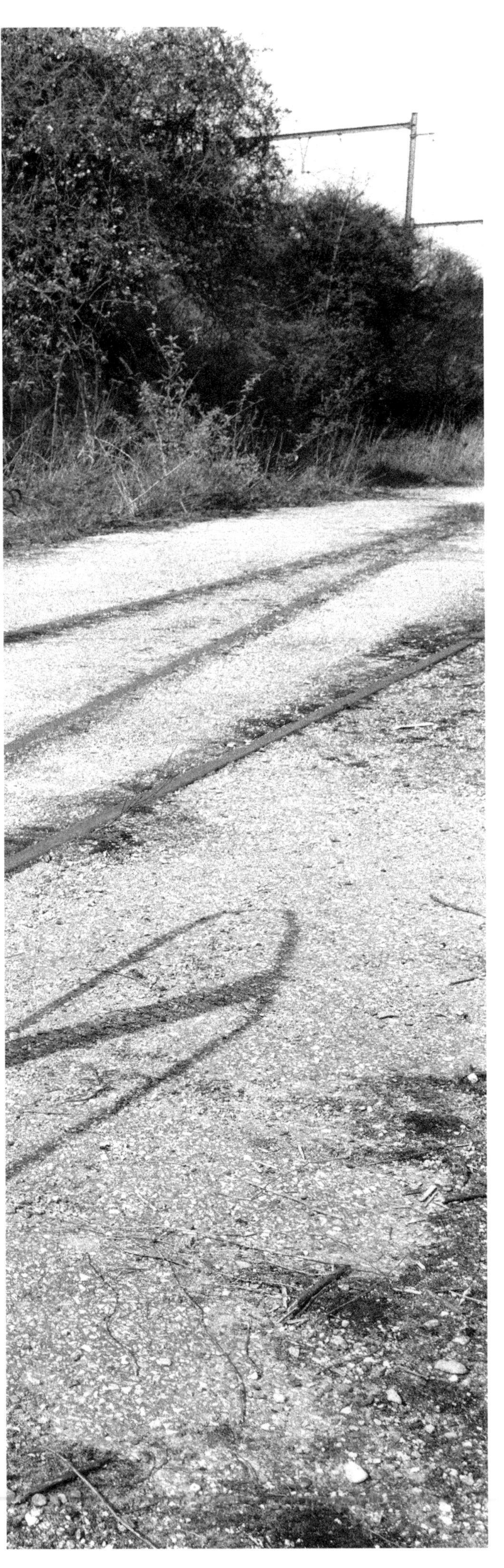

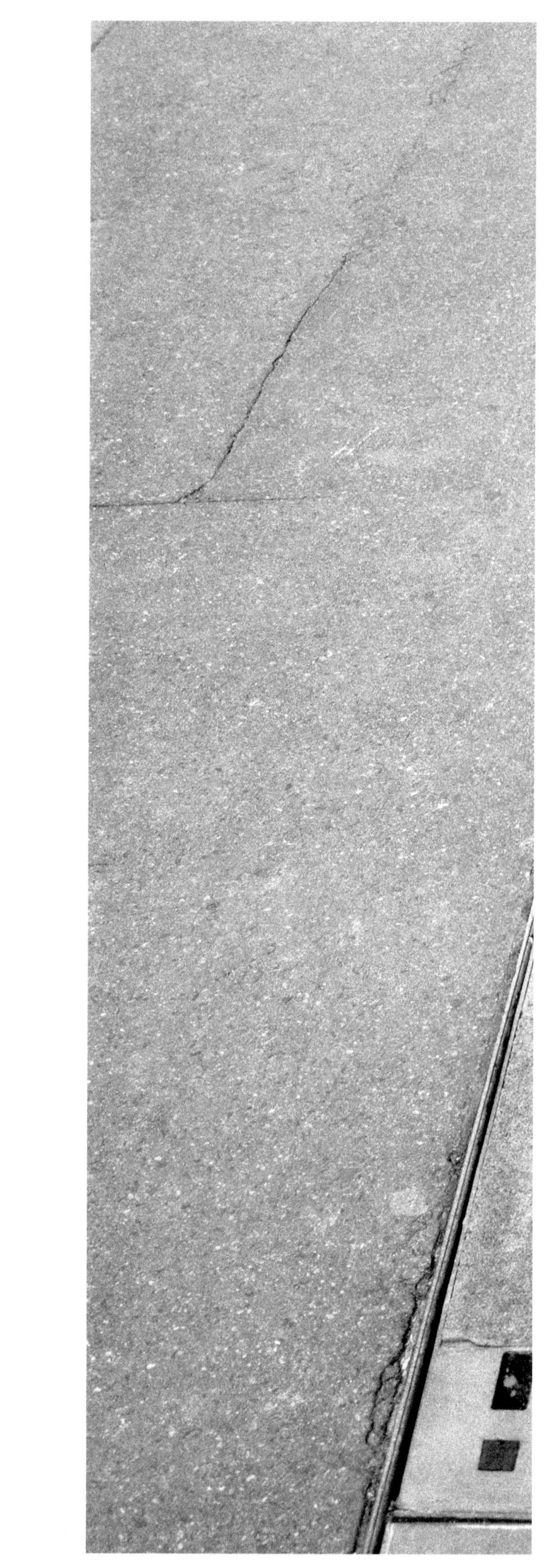

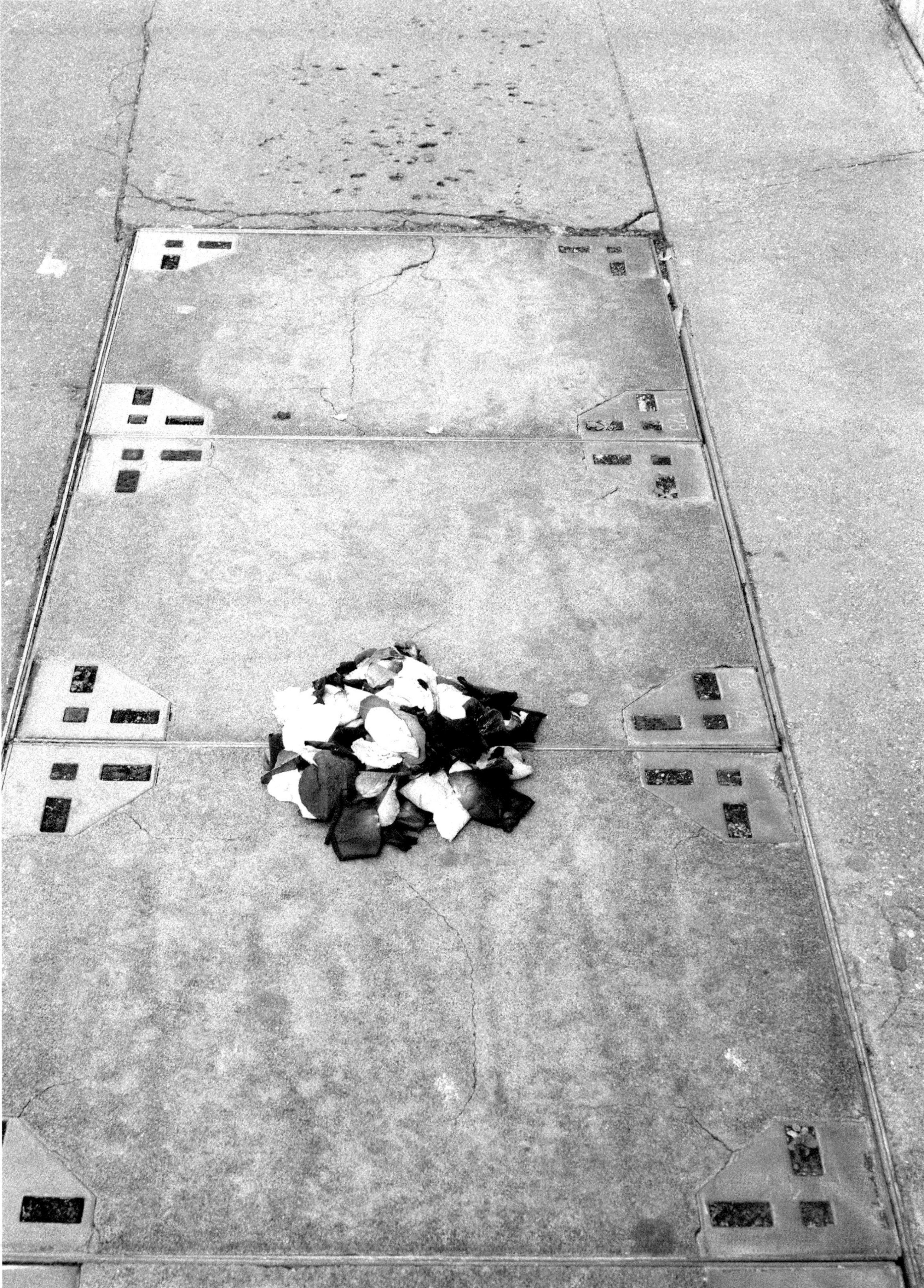

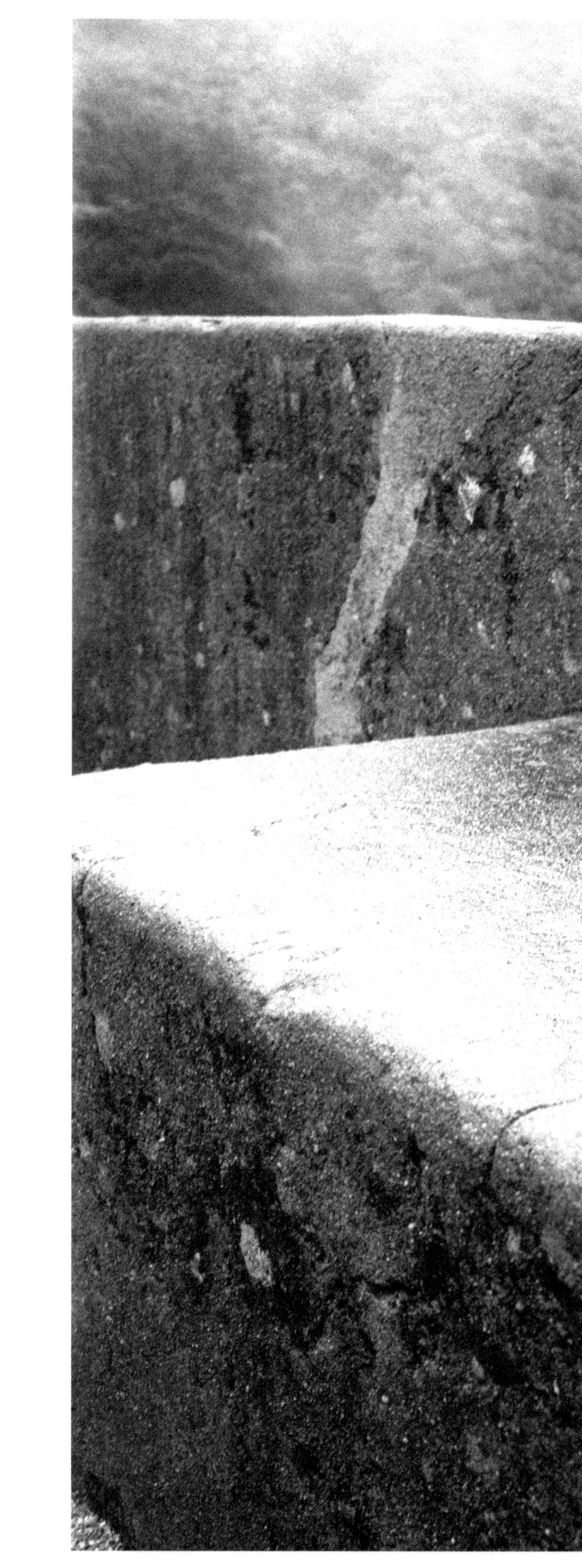

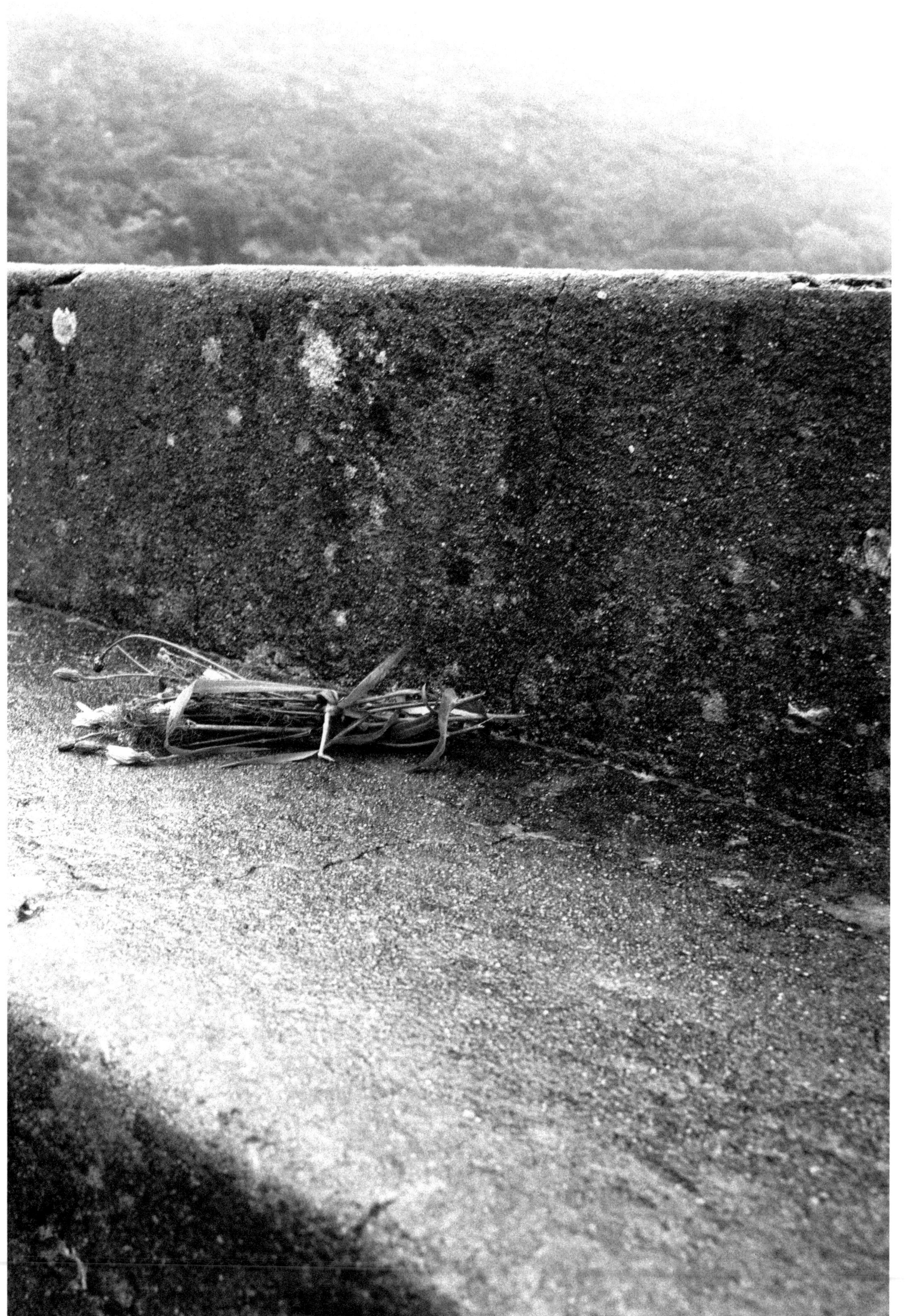

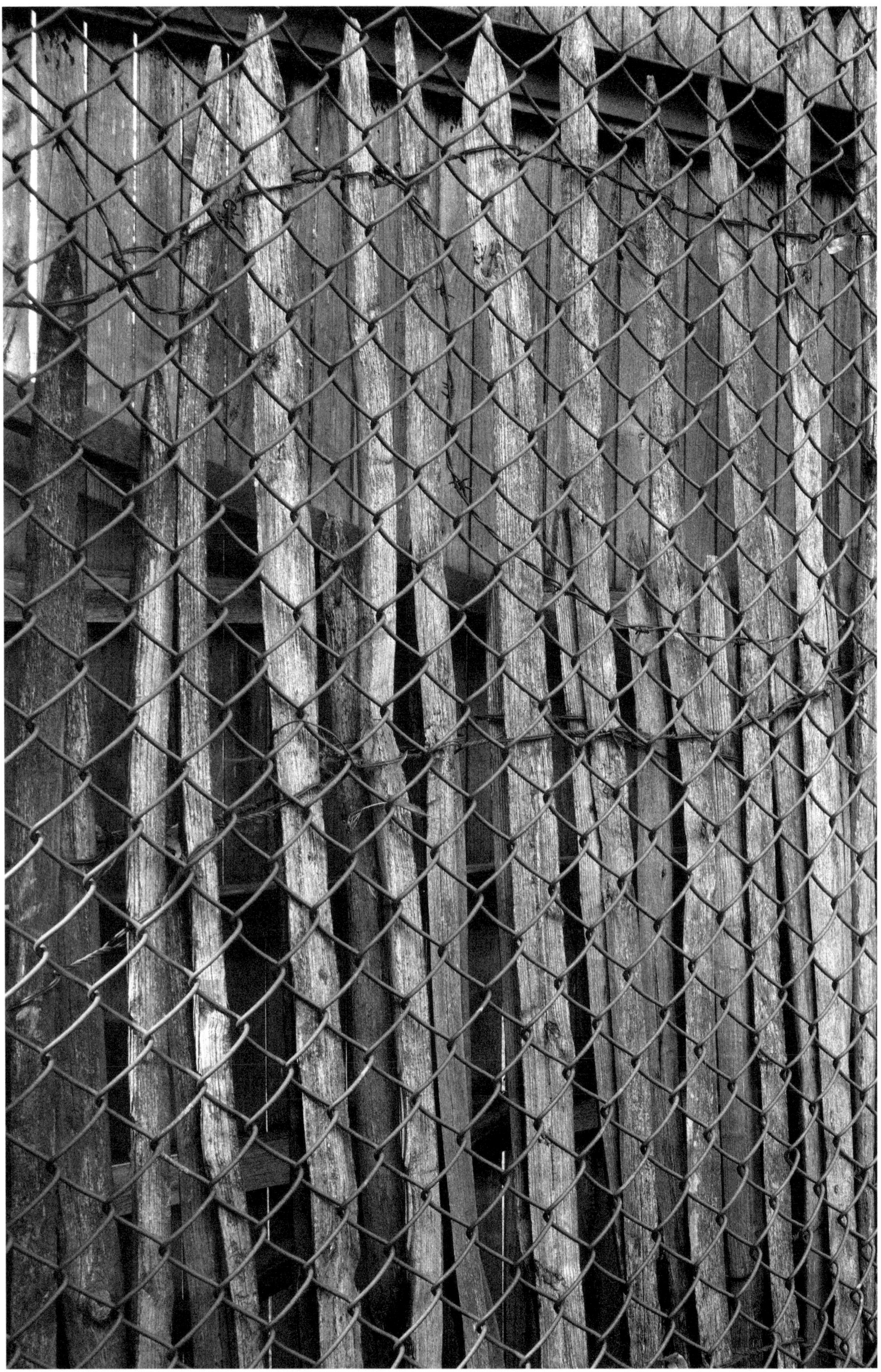

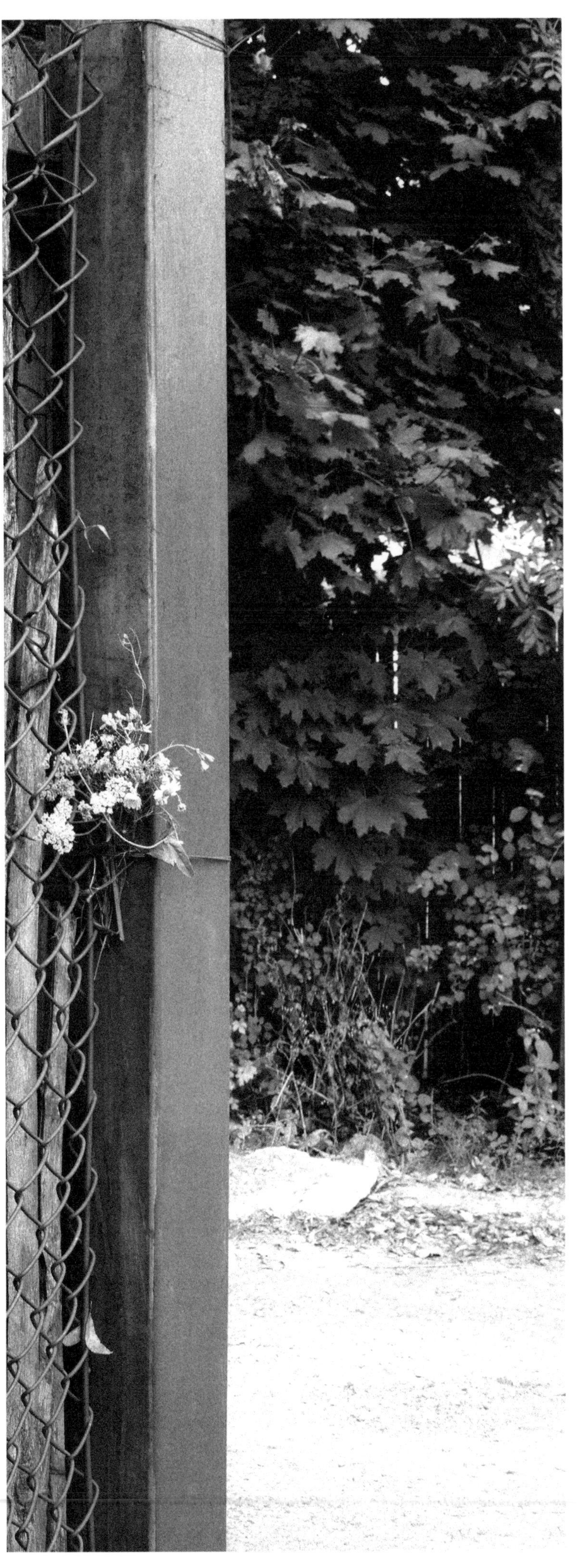

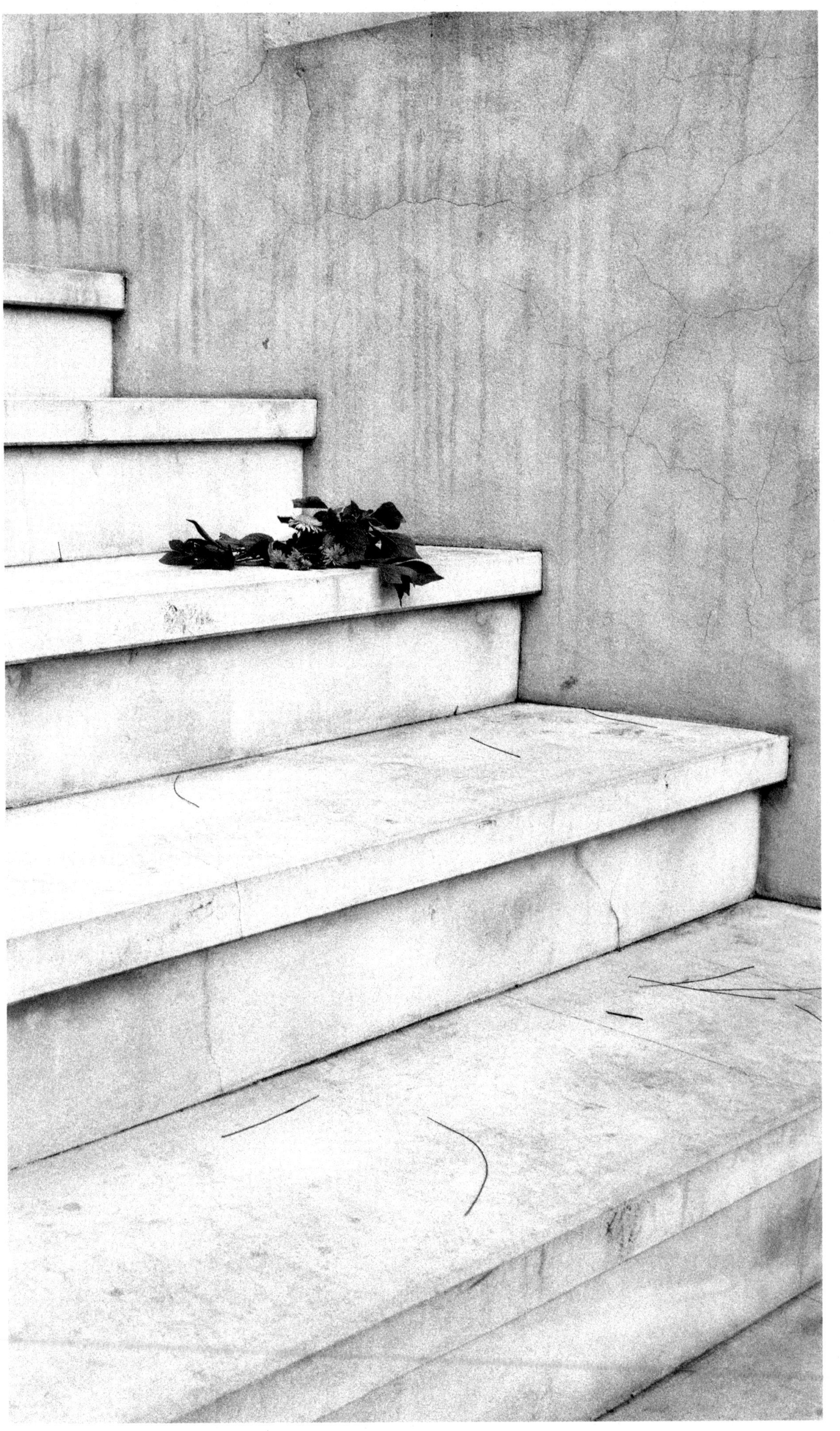

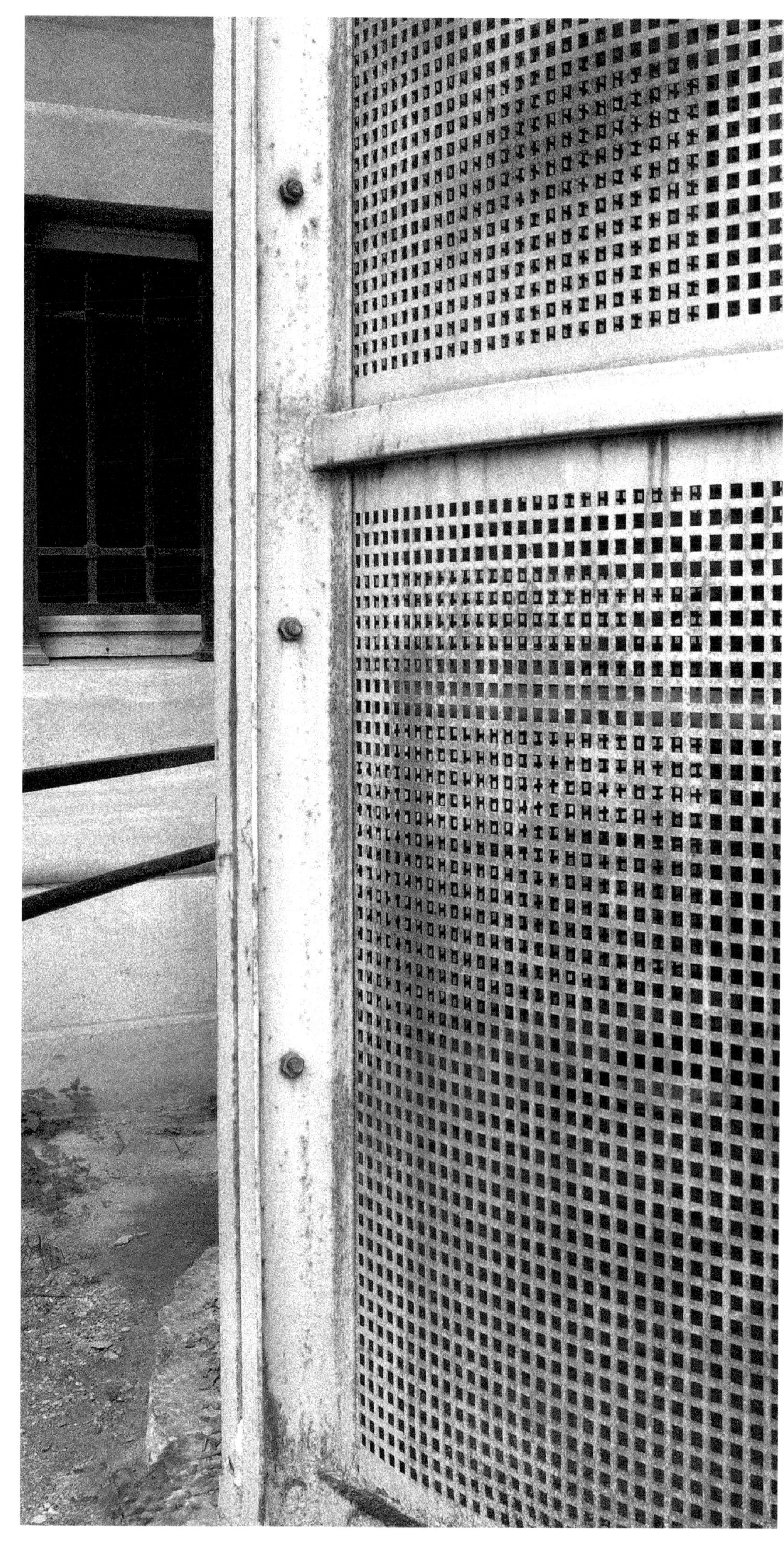

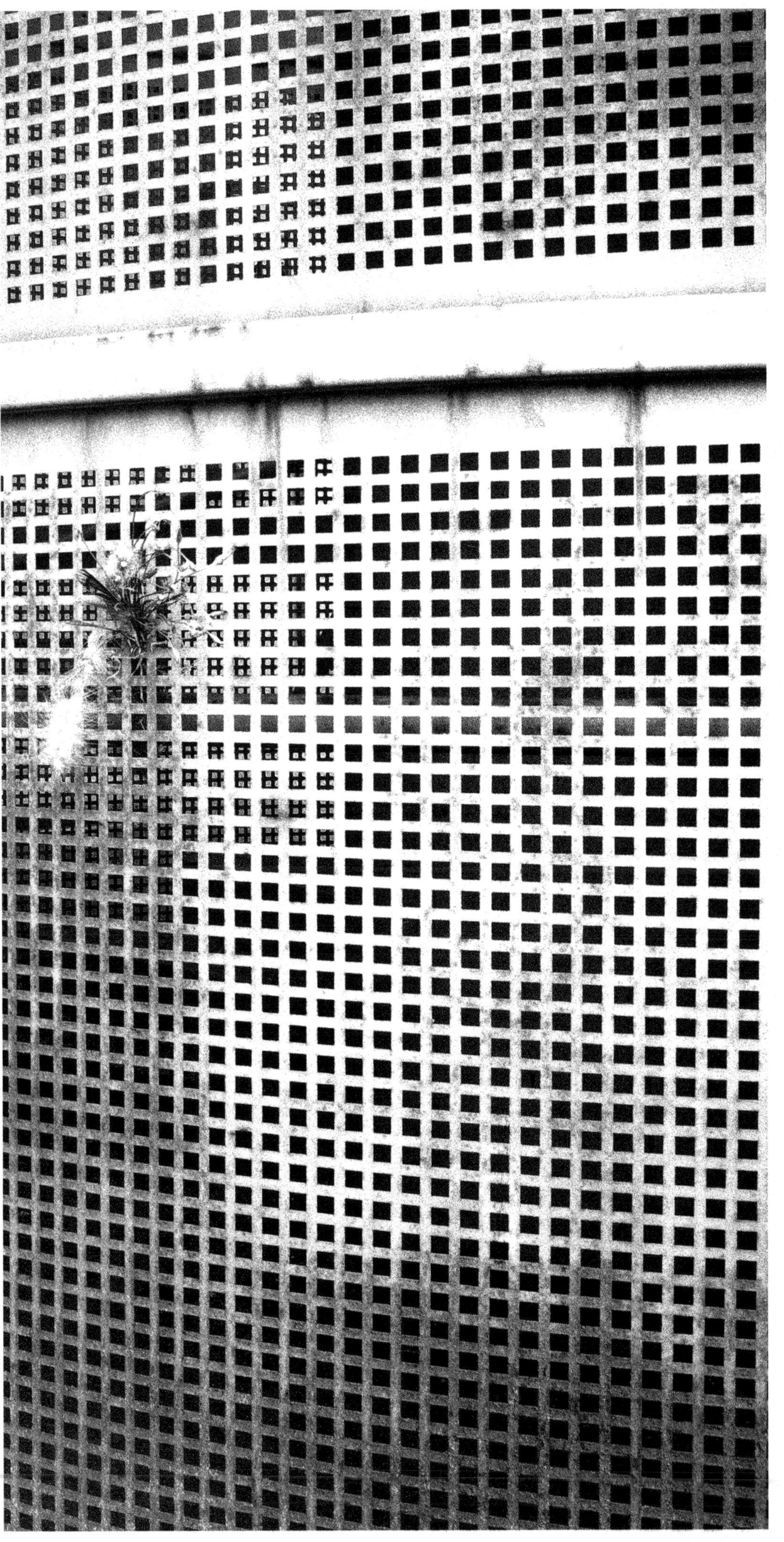

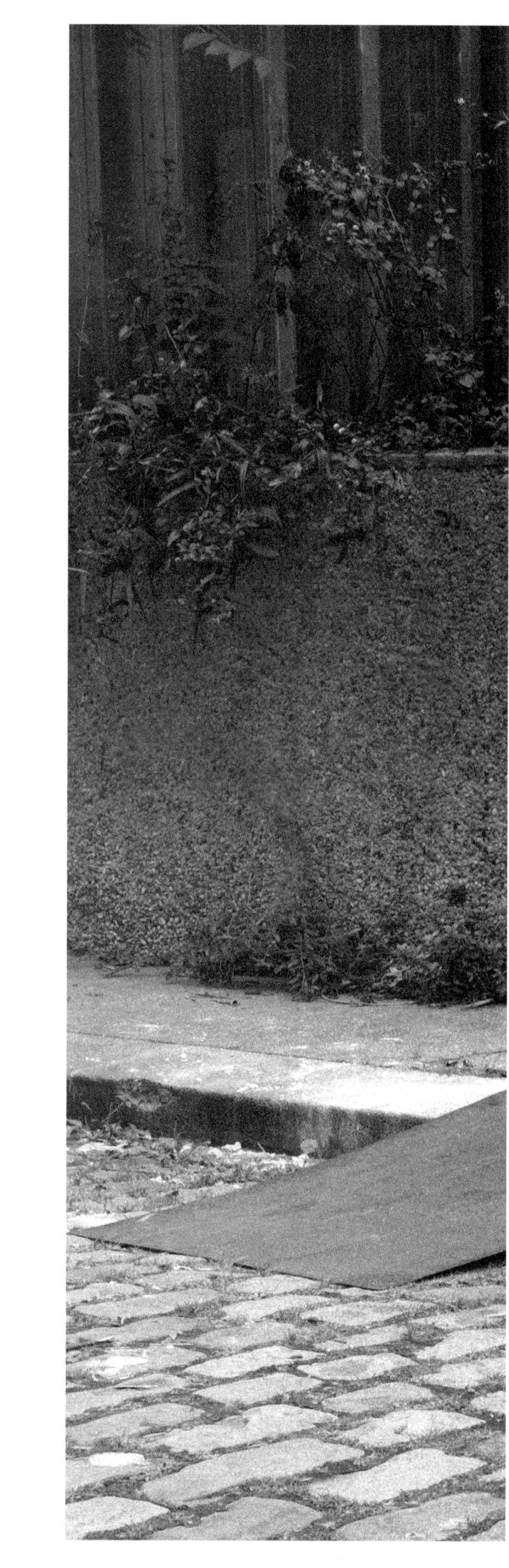

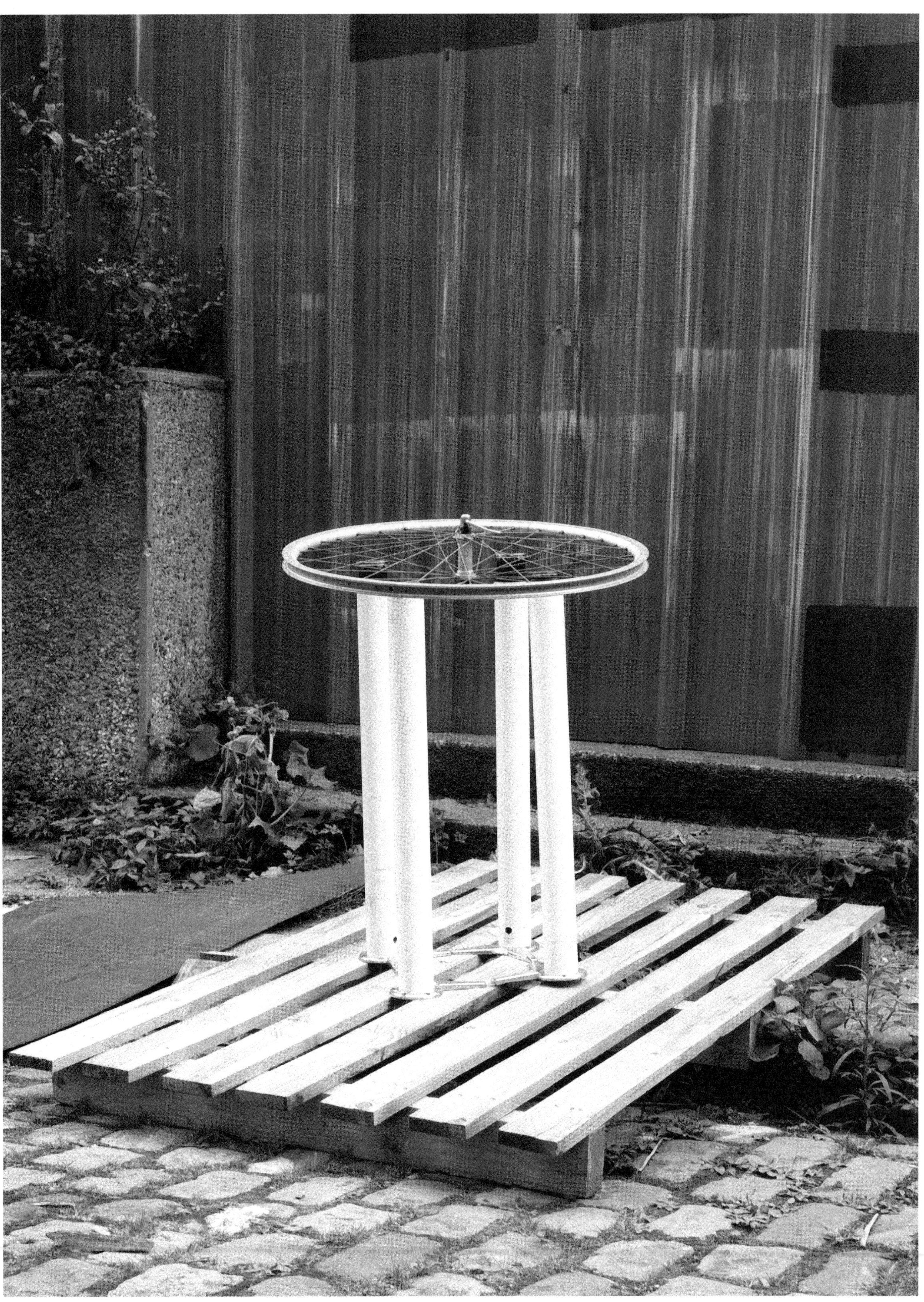

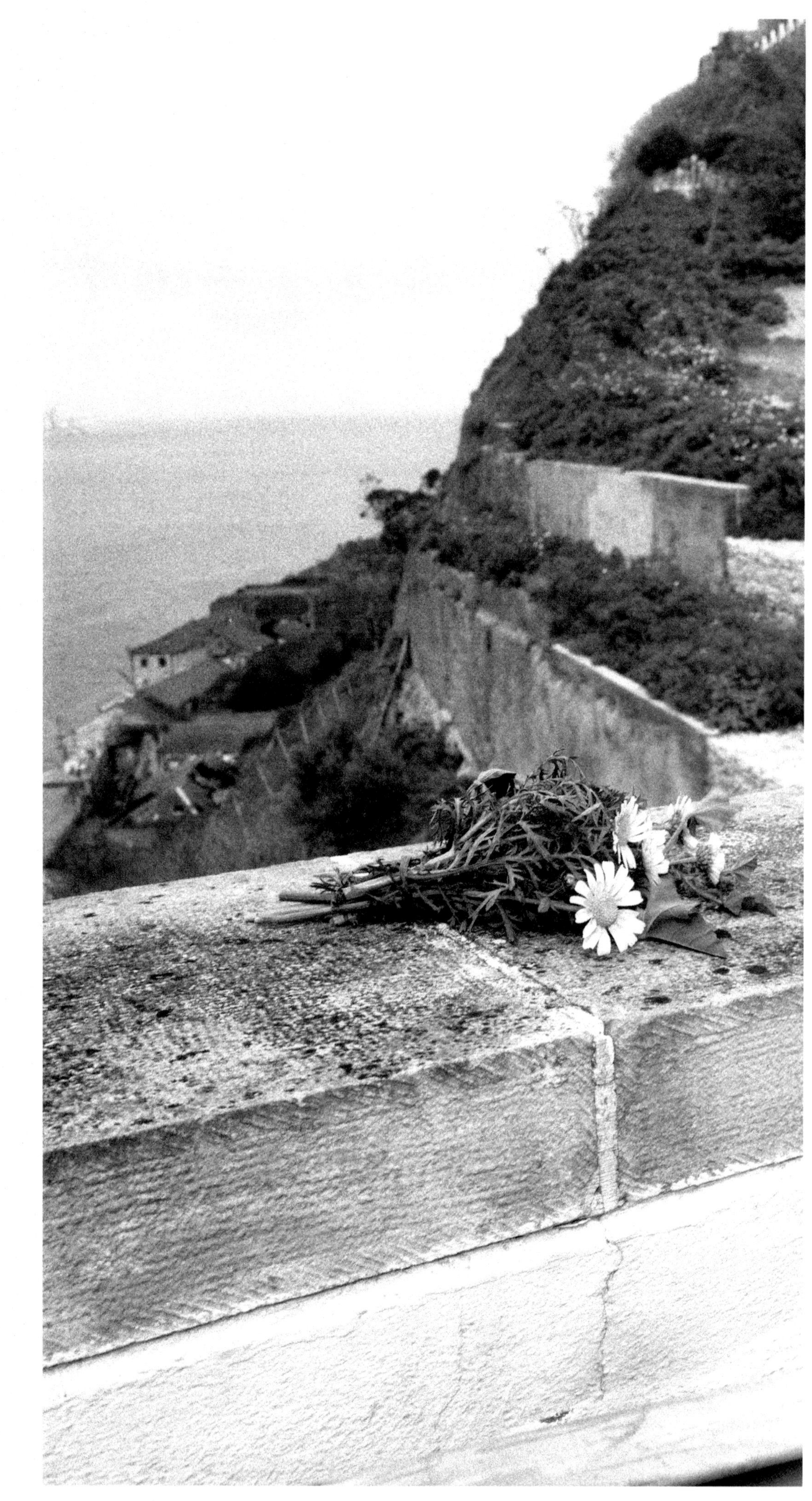

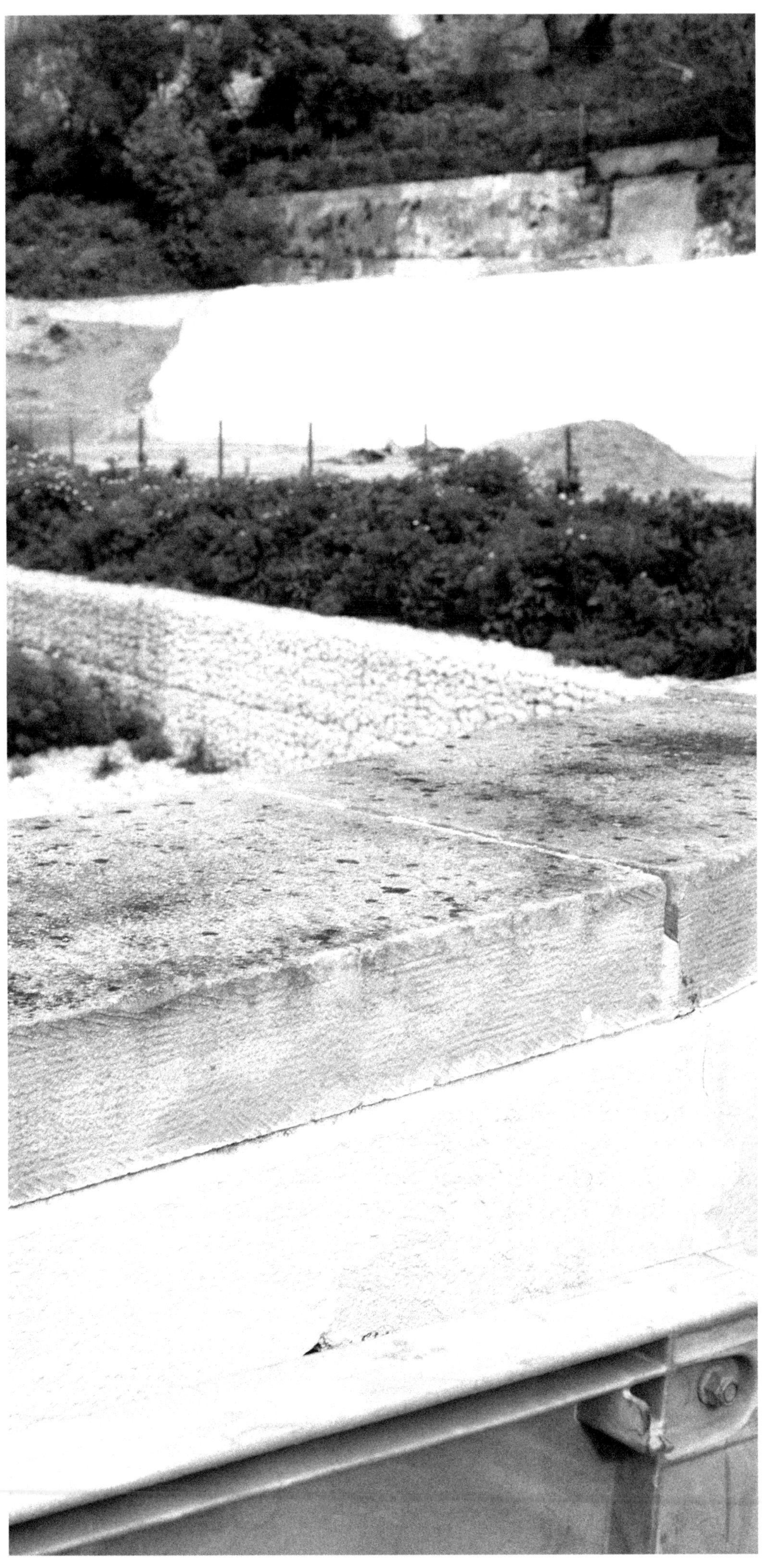

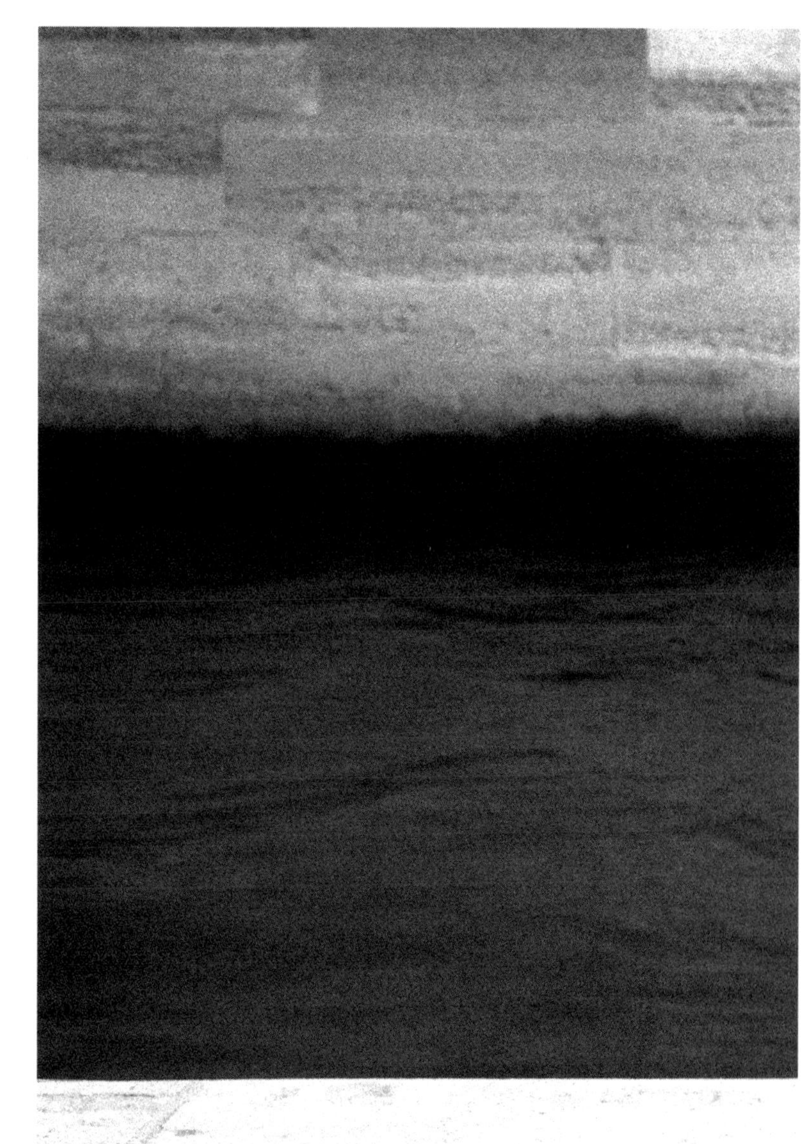
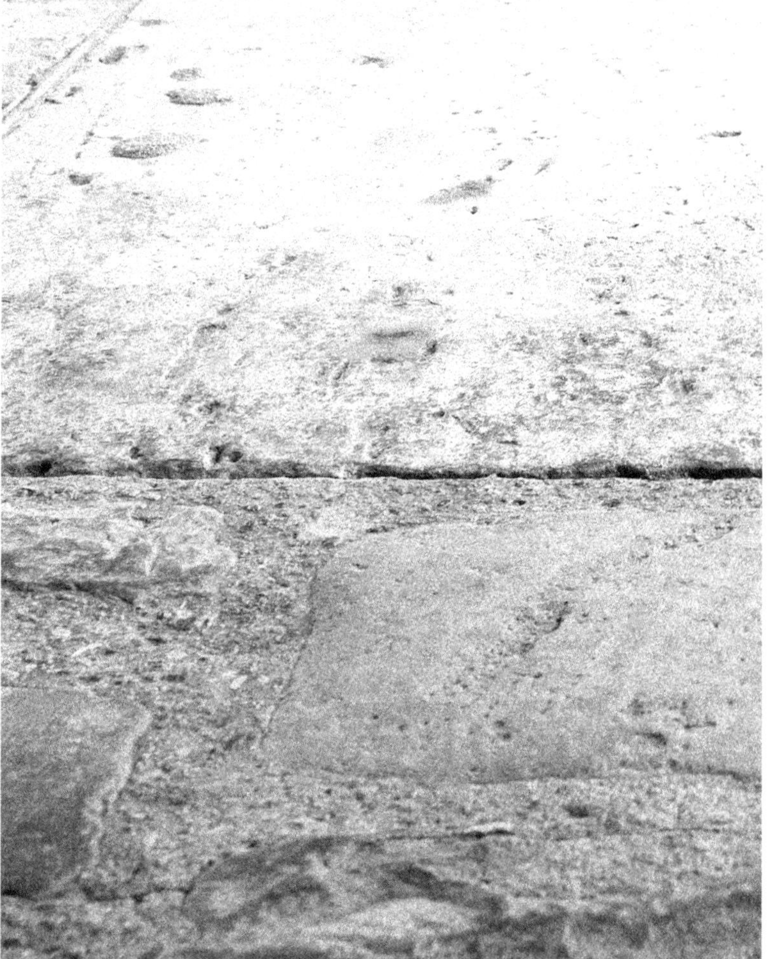

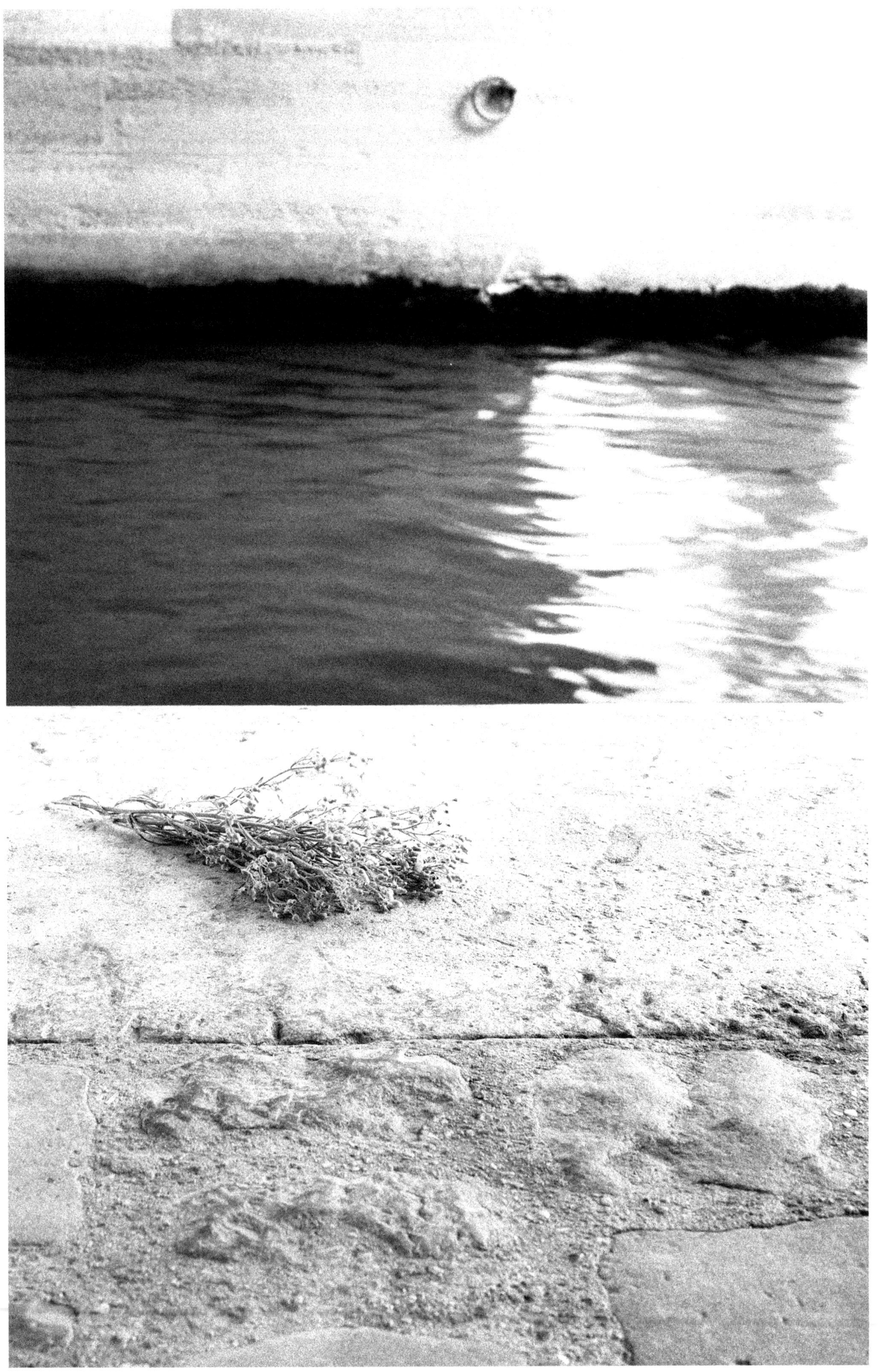

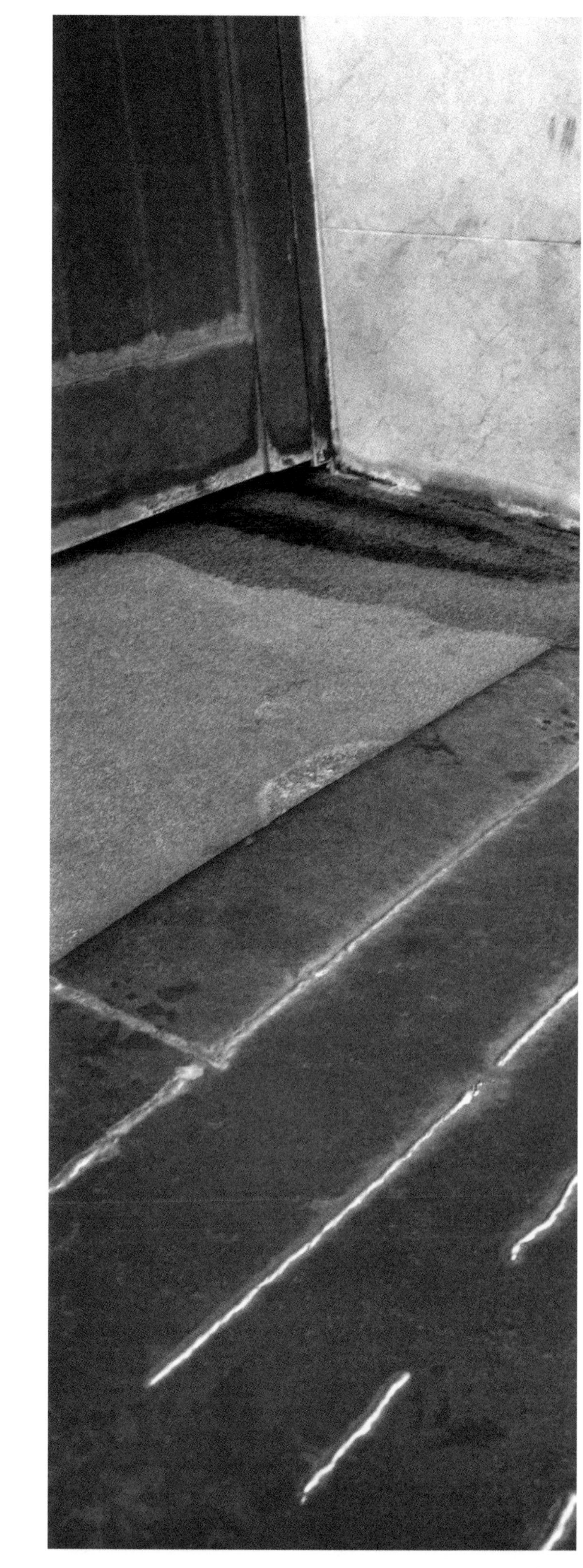

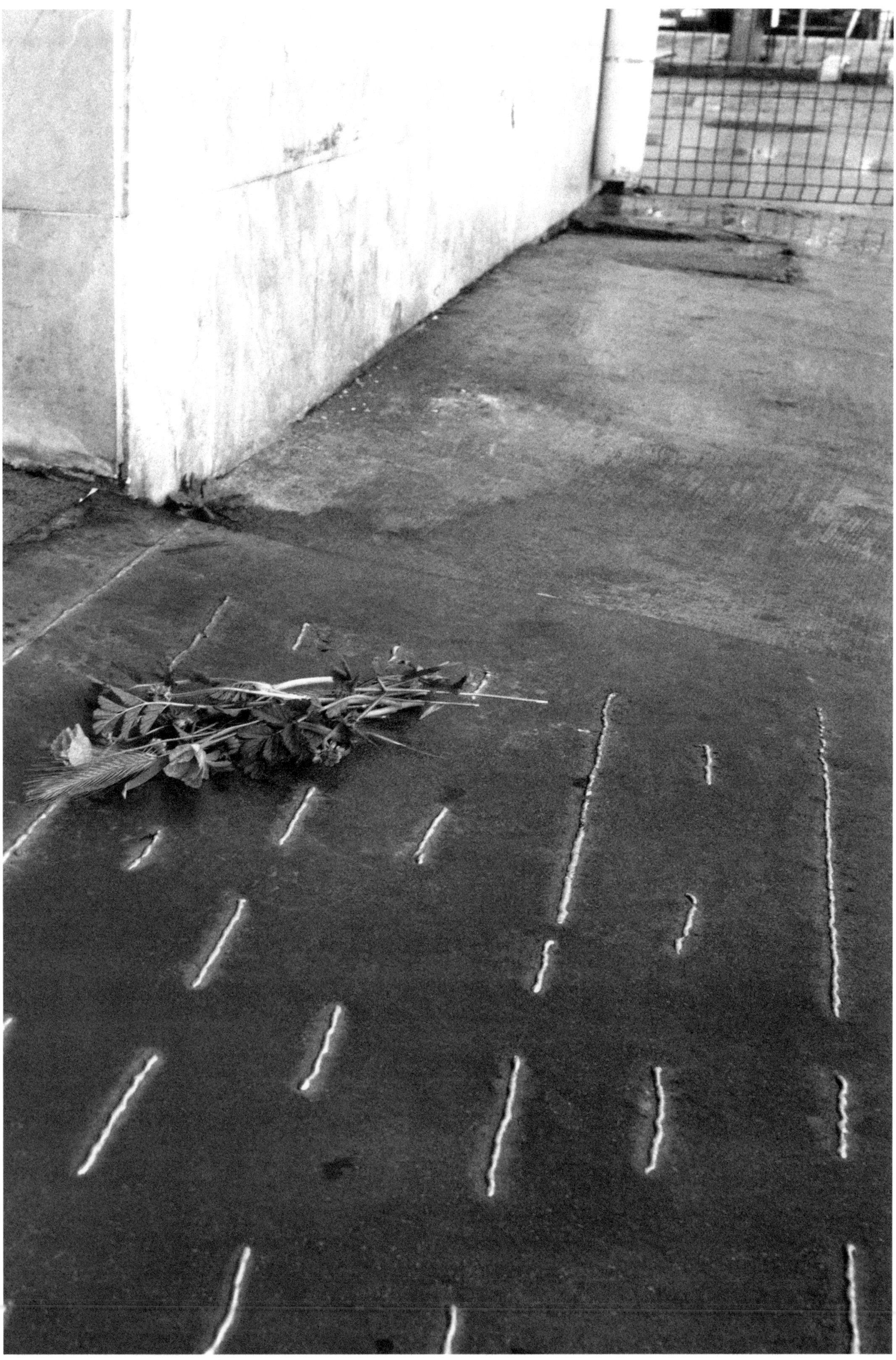

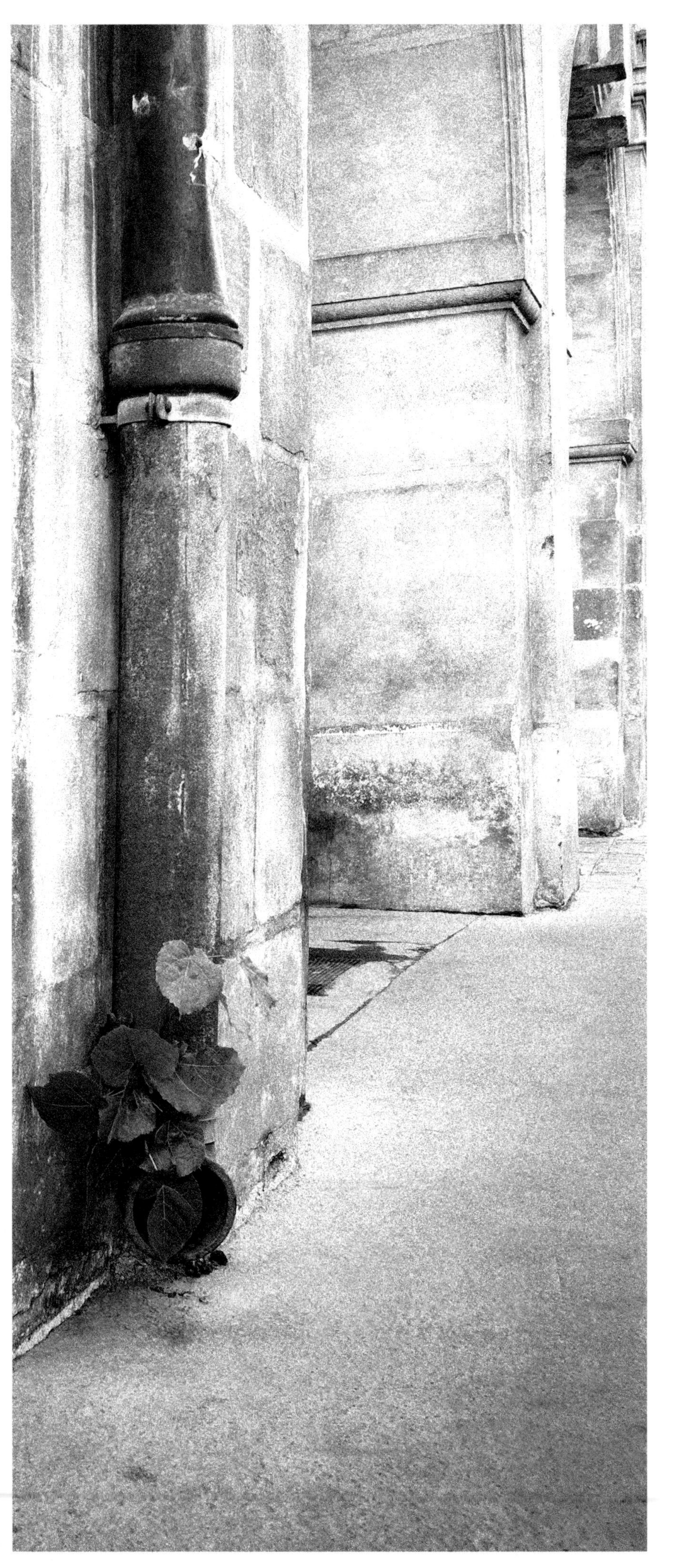

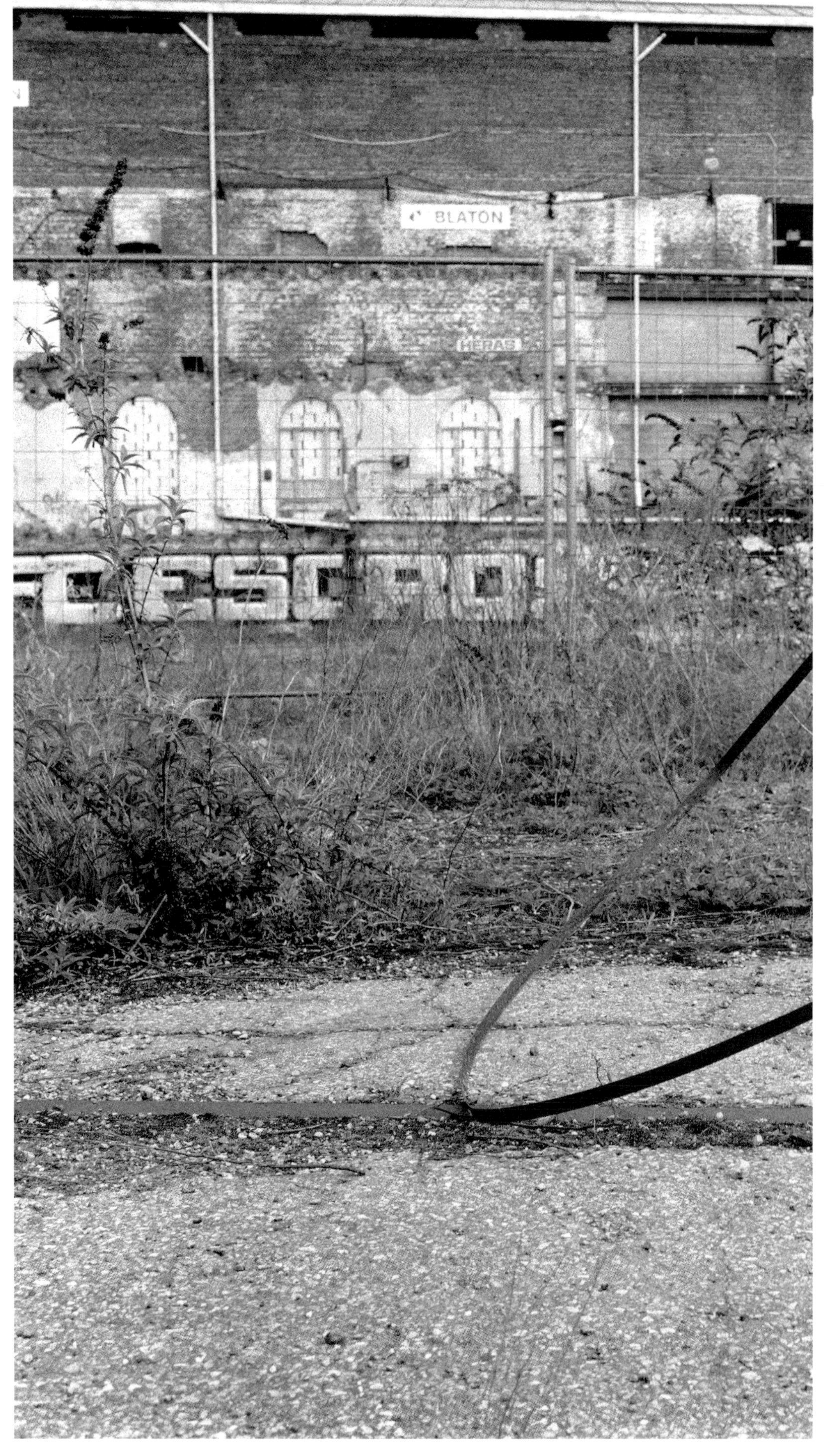
BLATON
HERAS

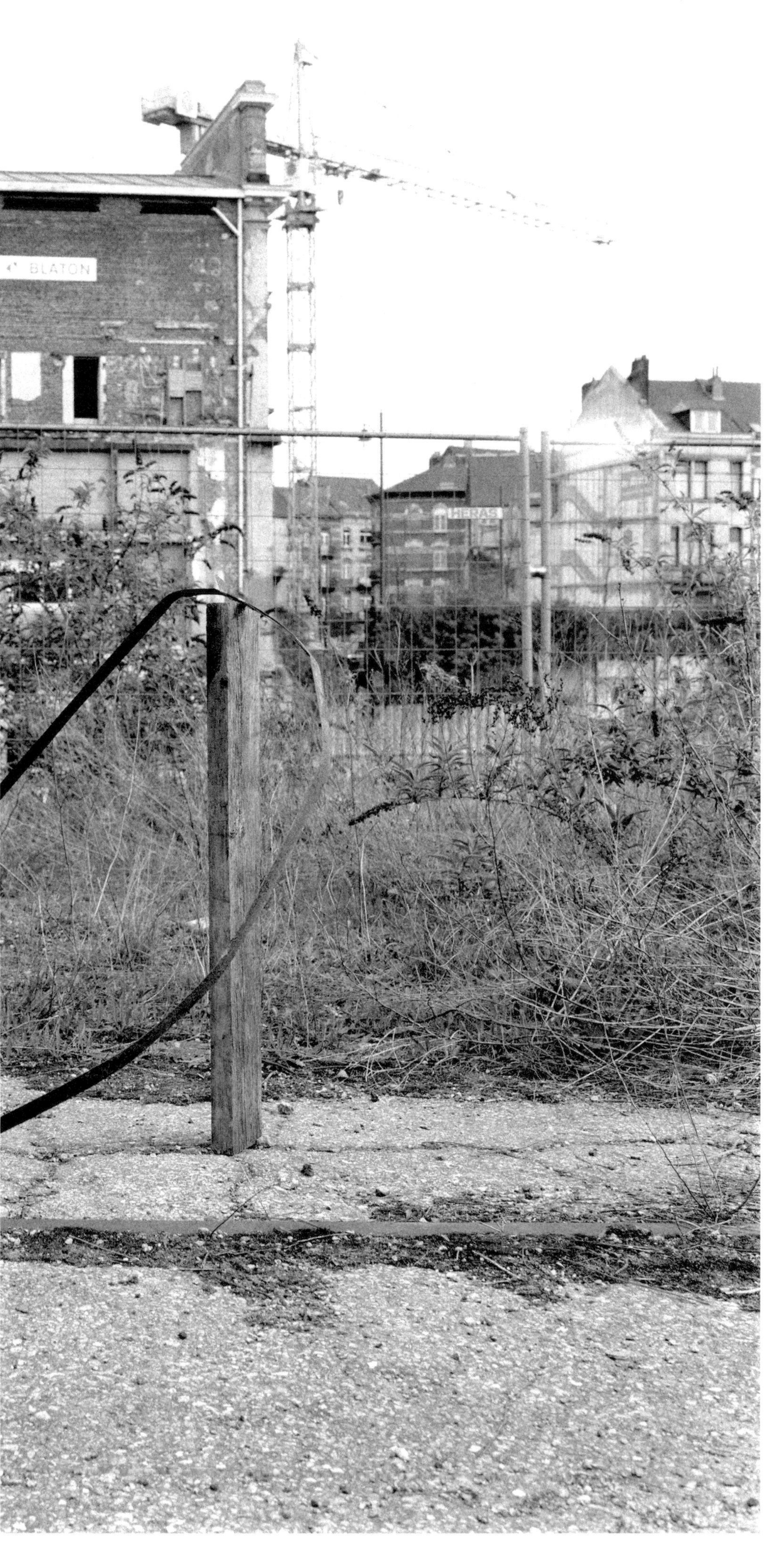
BLATON
HERAS

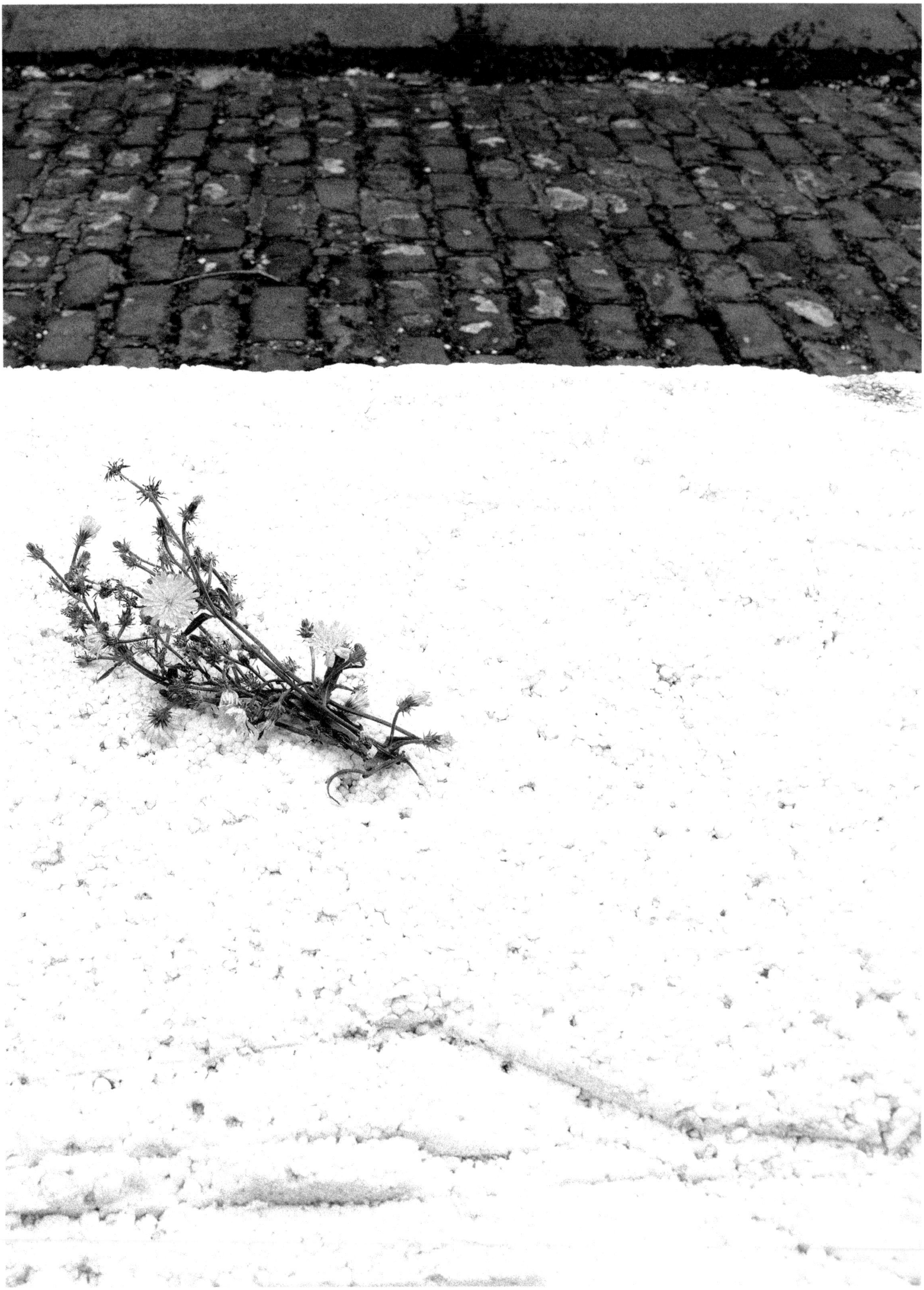

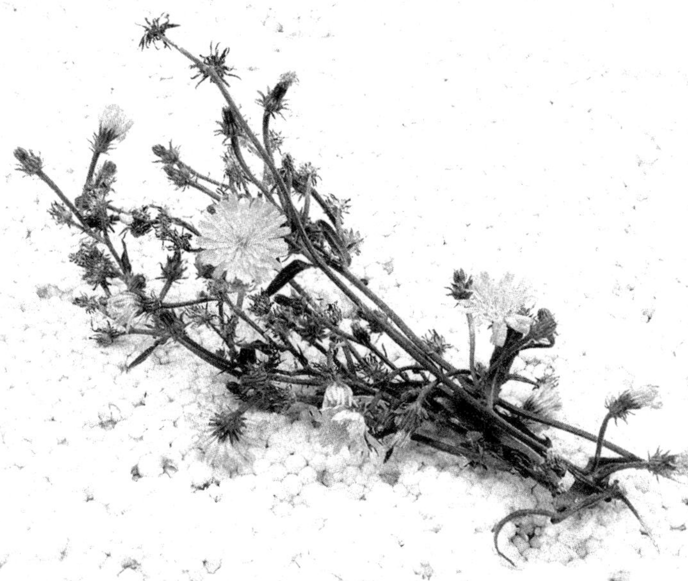

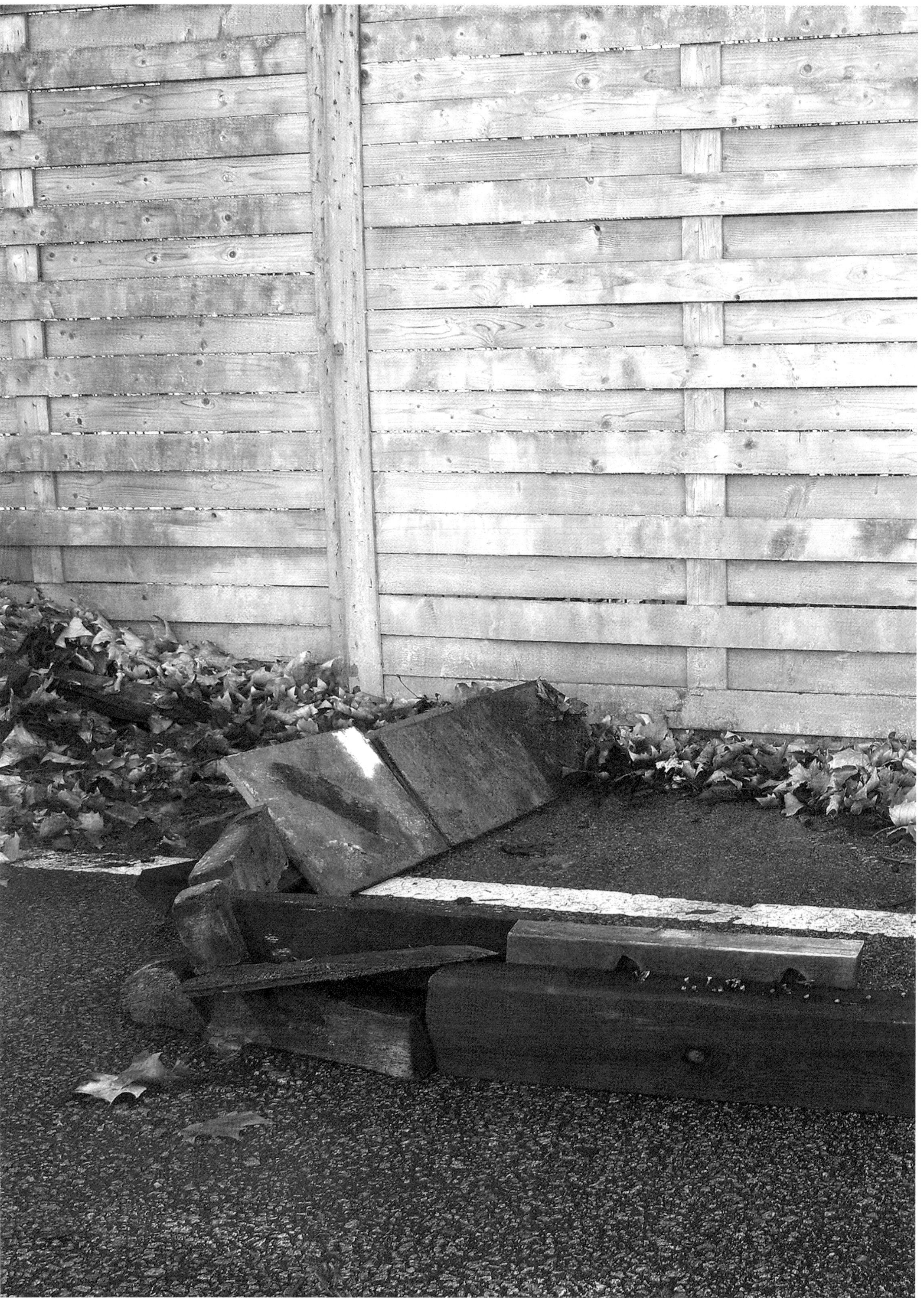

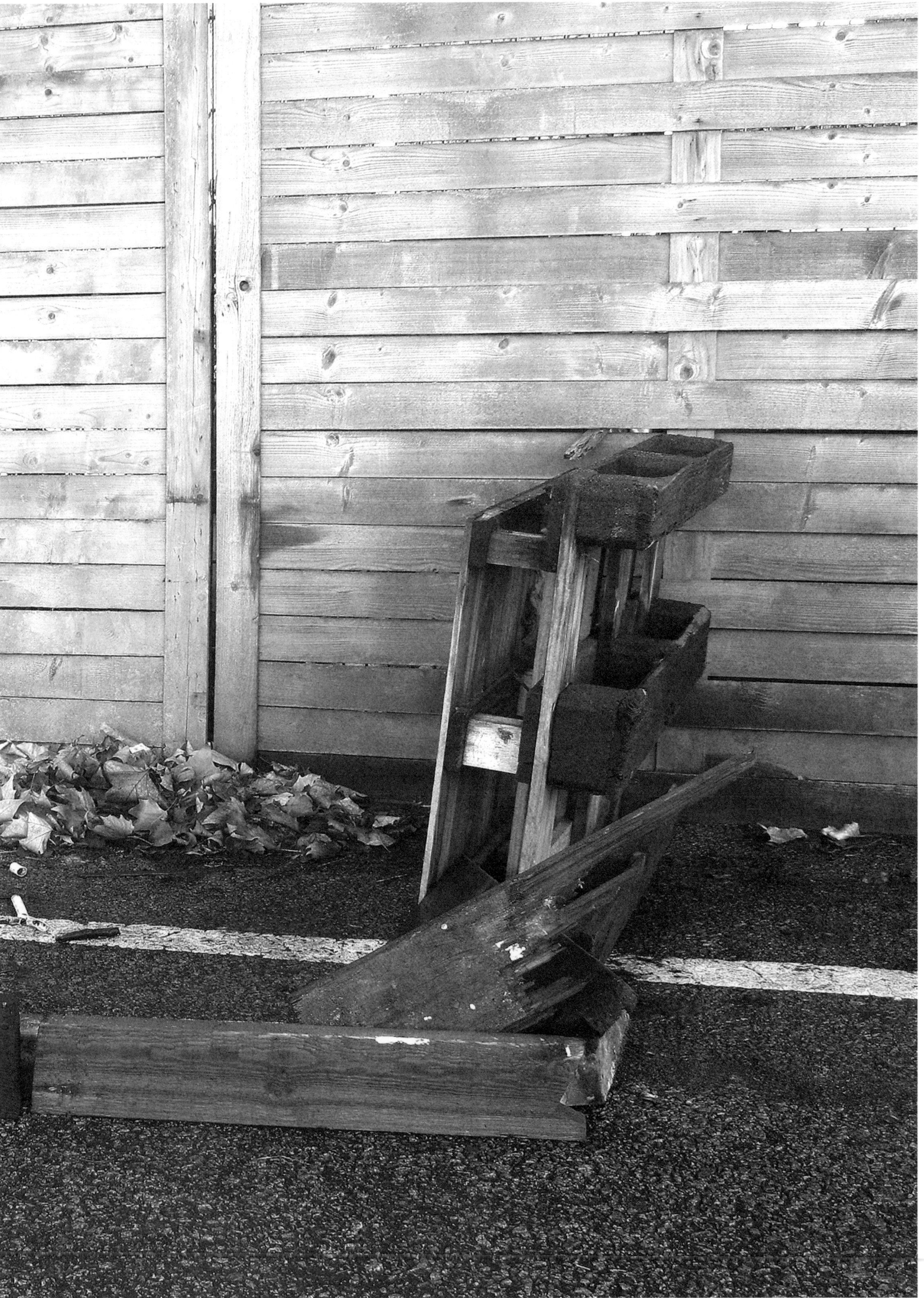

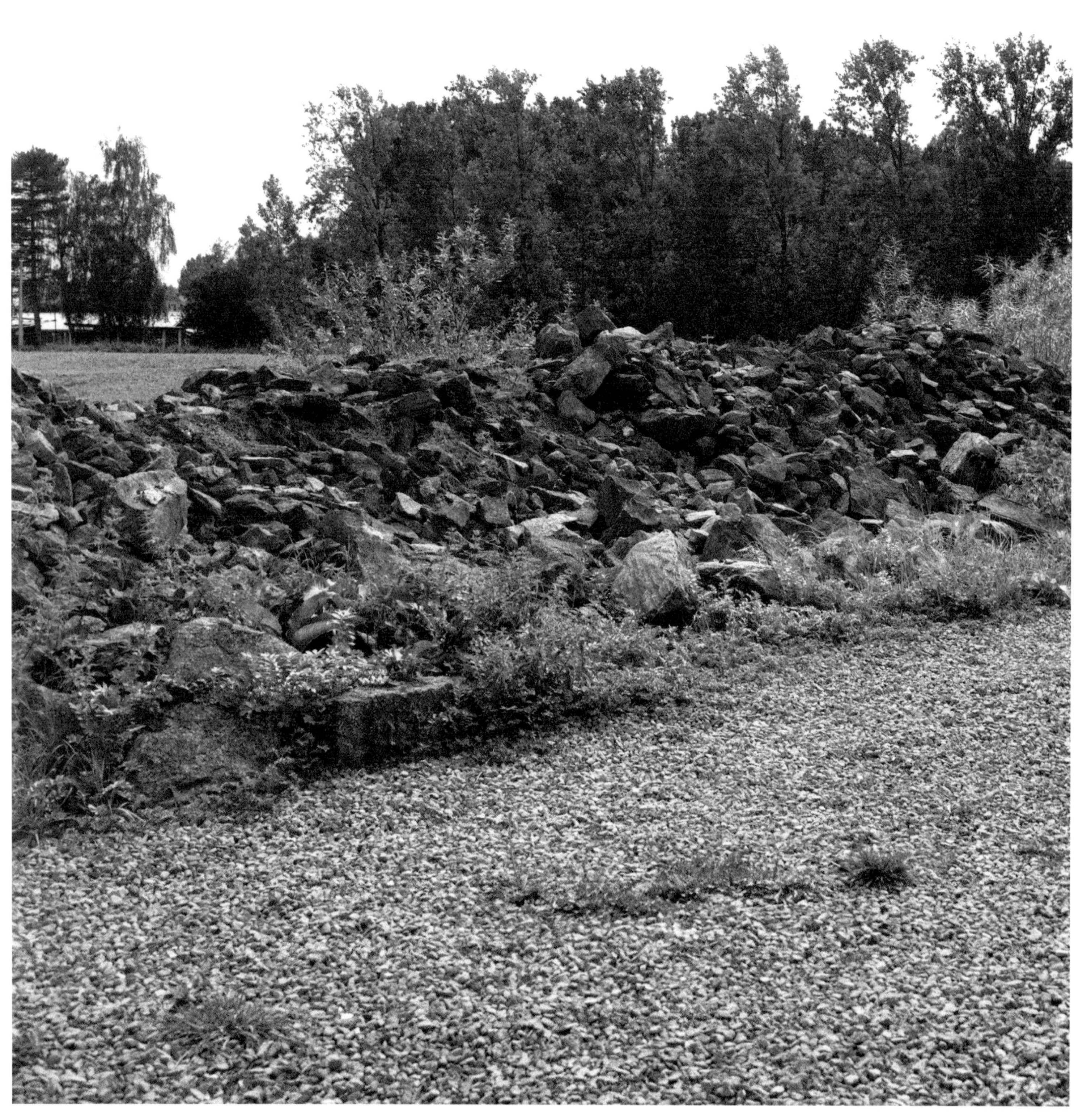

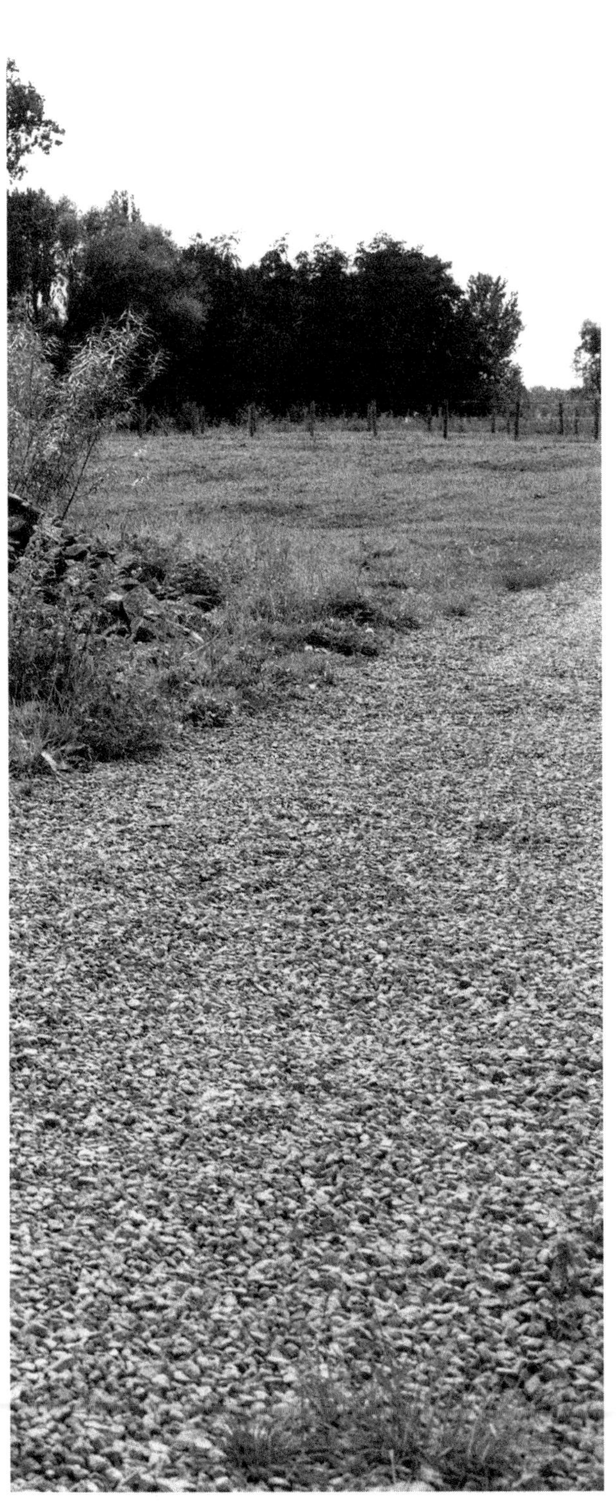

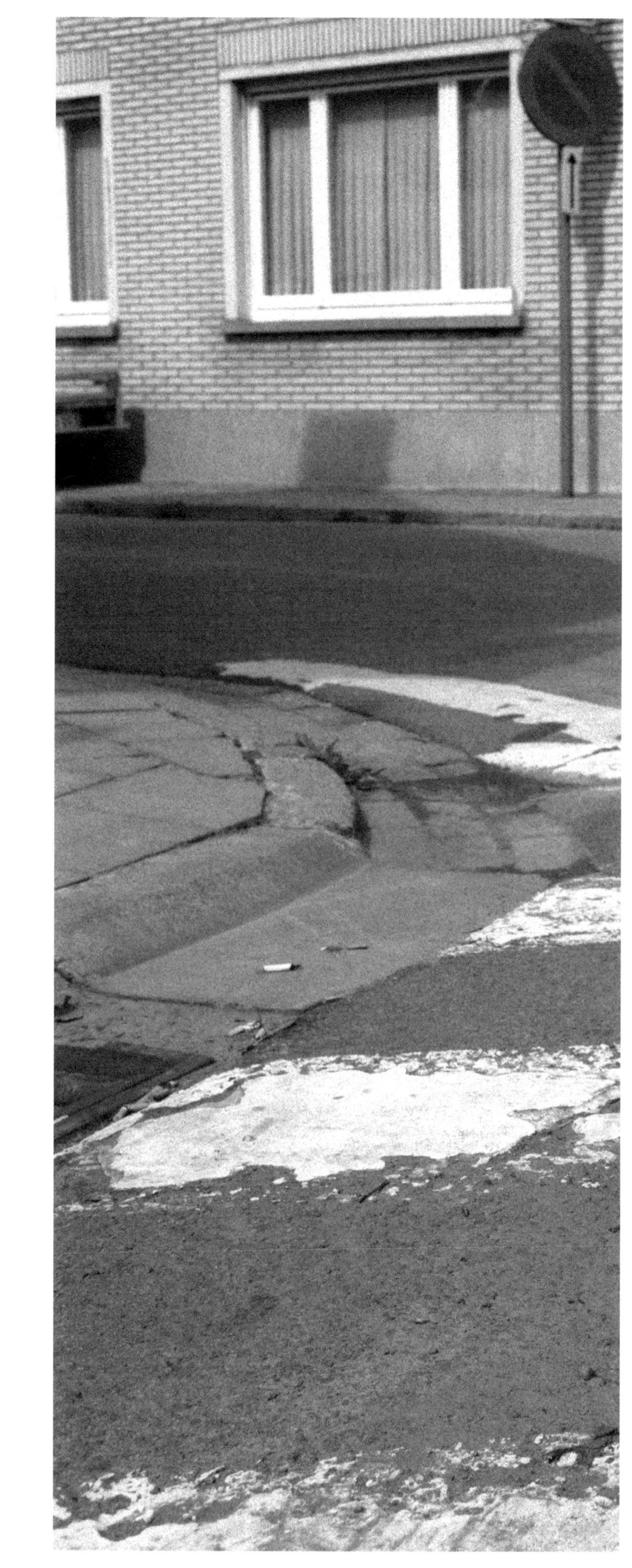

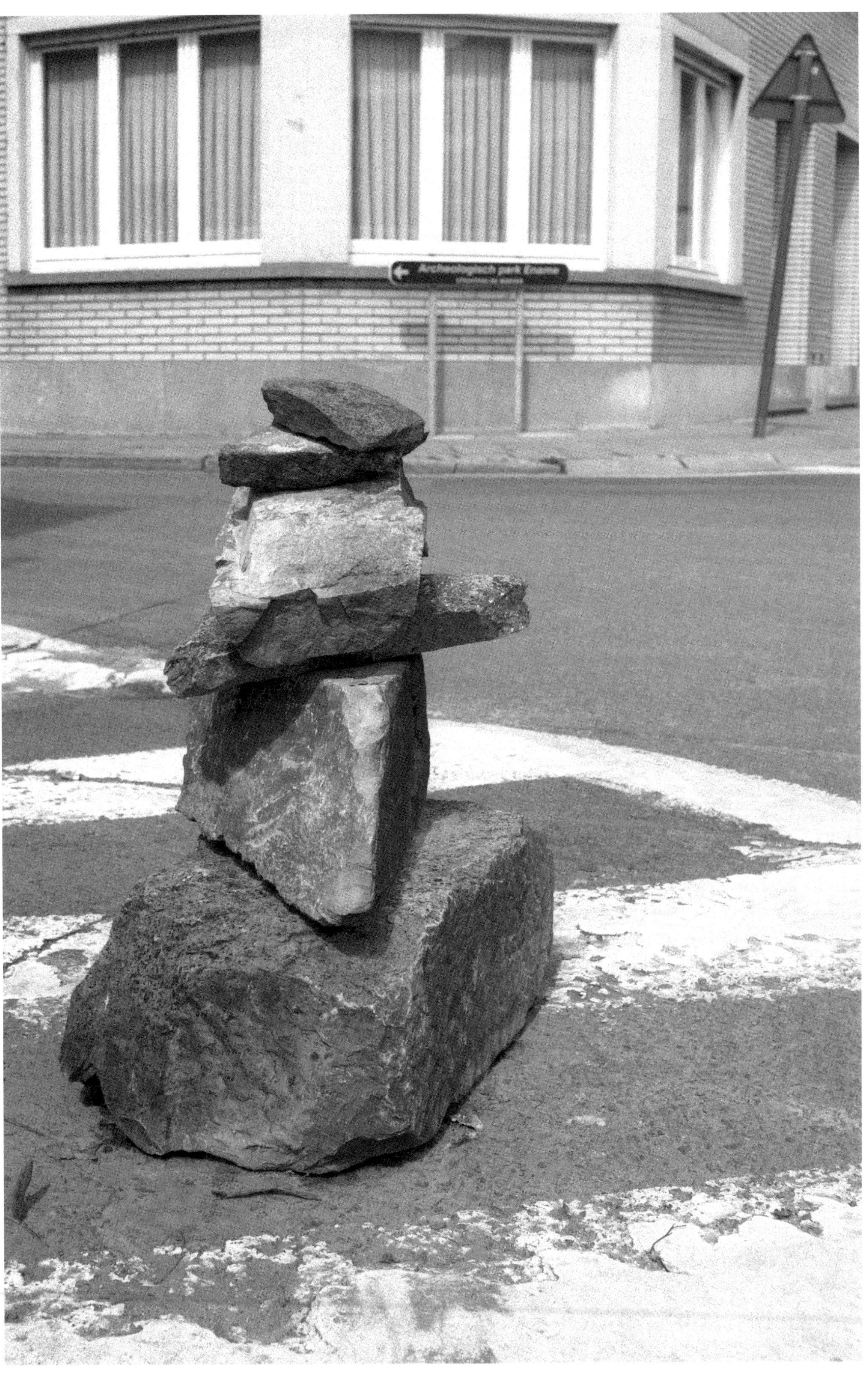
Archeologisch park Ename

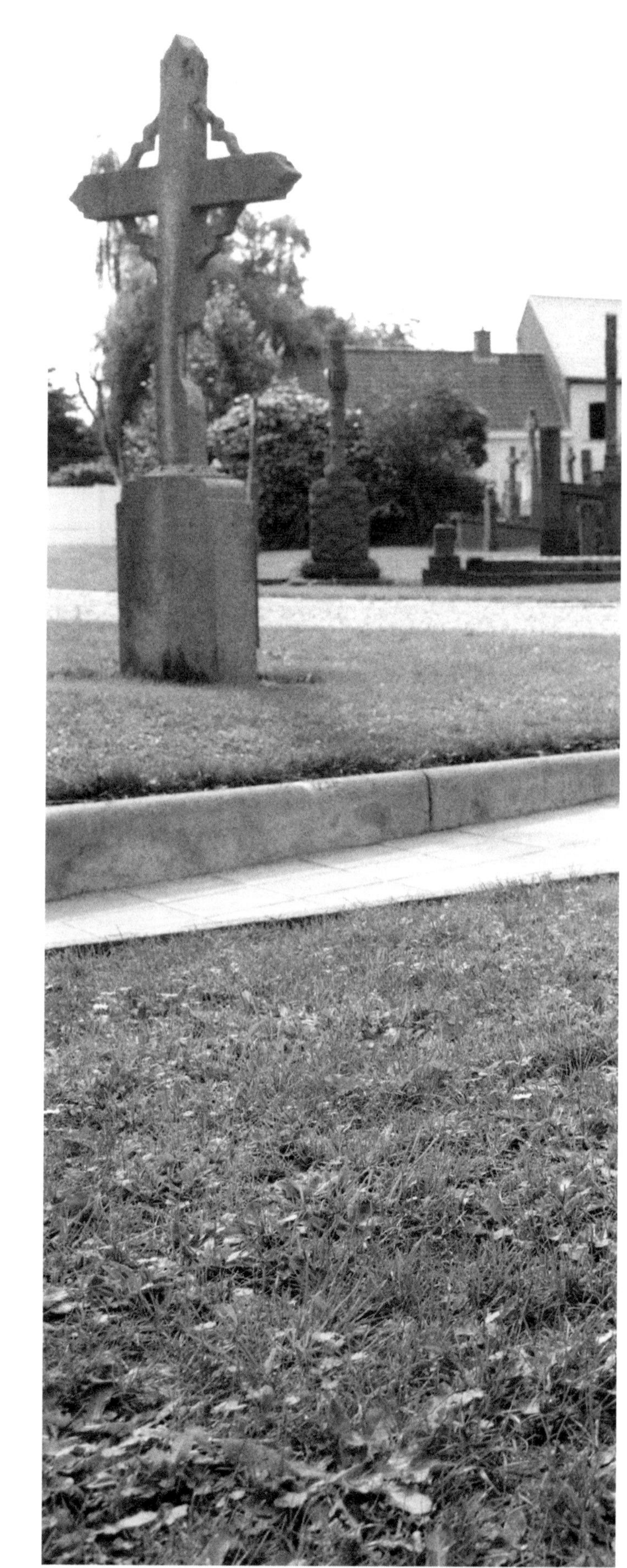

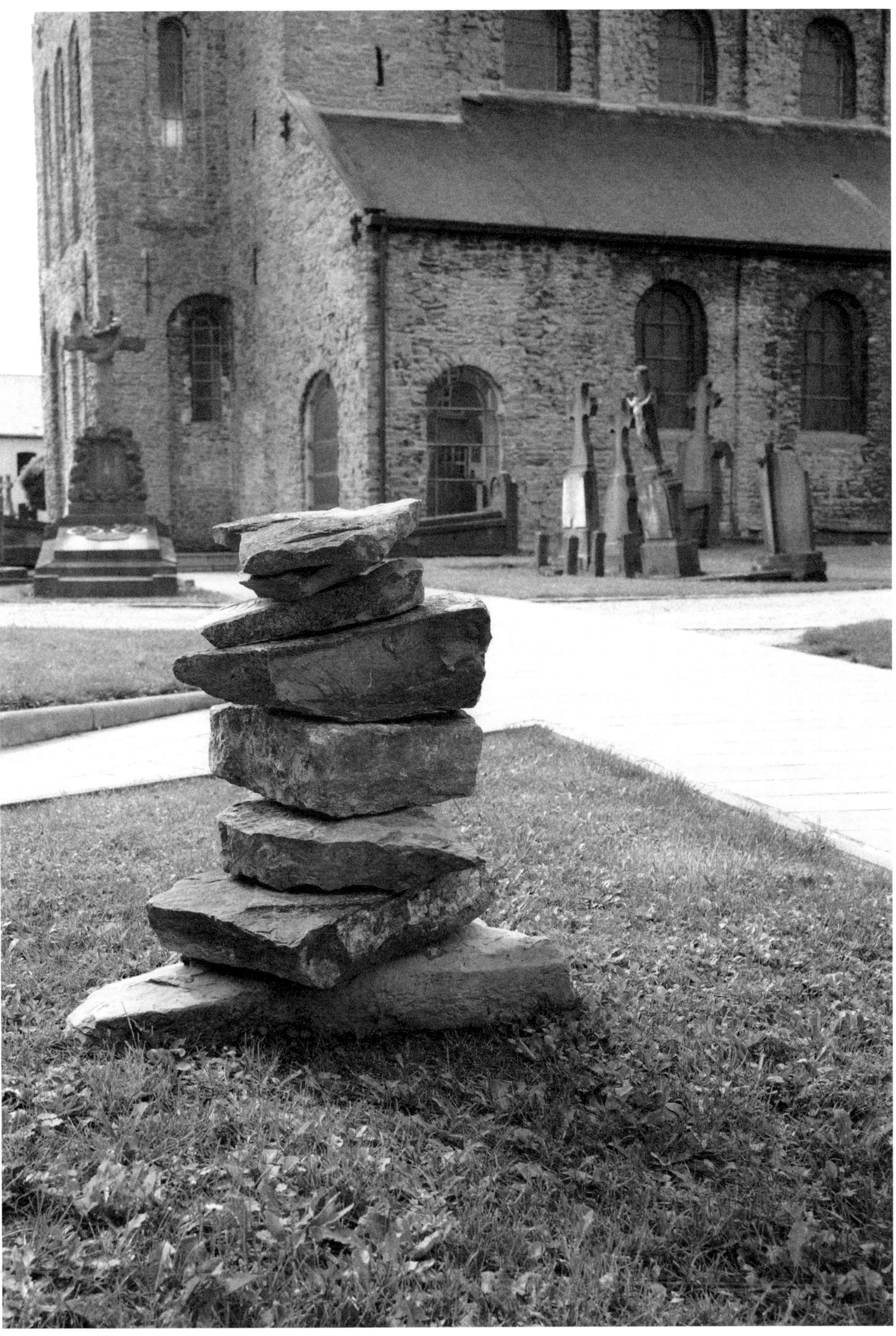

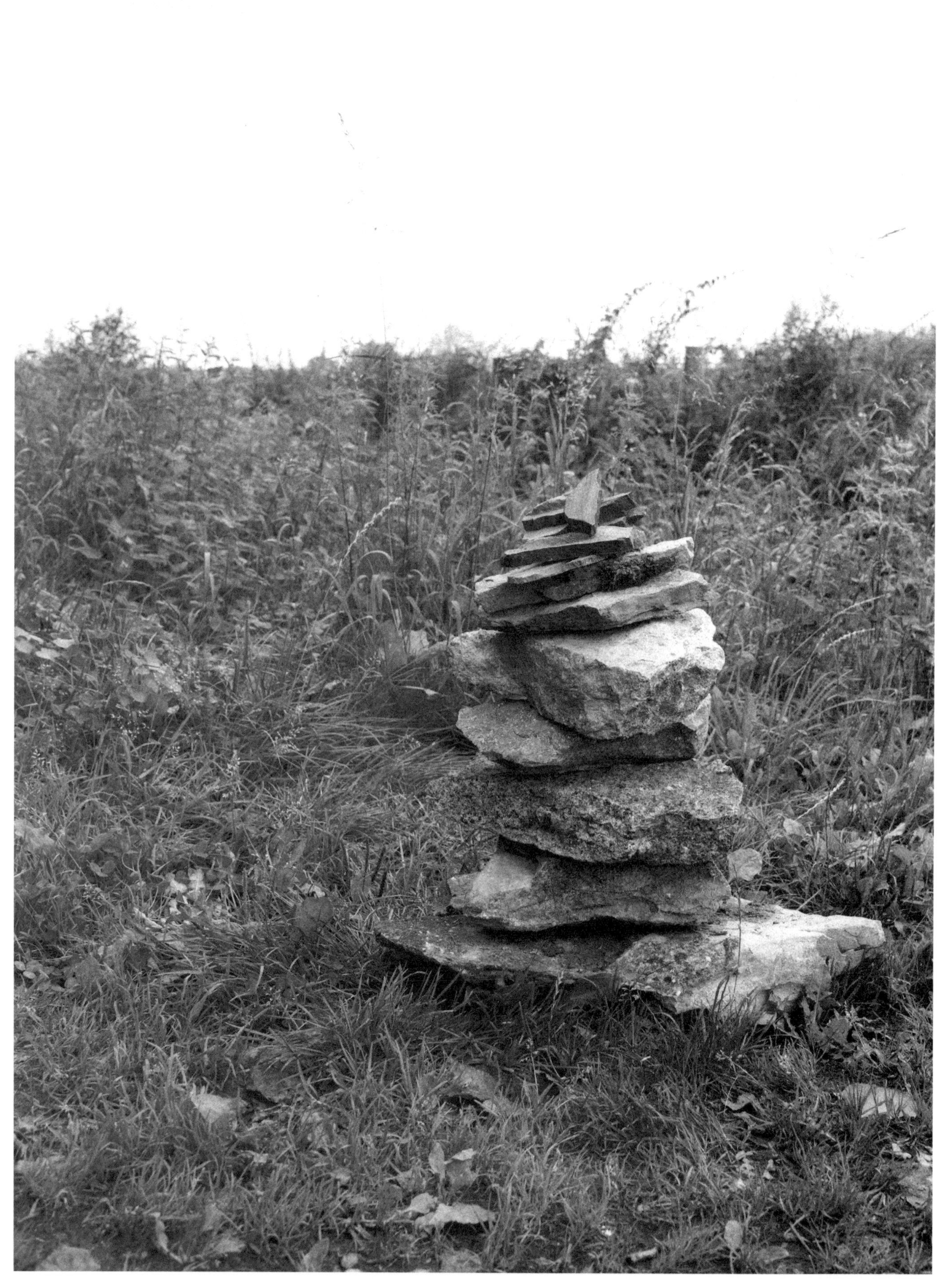

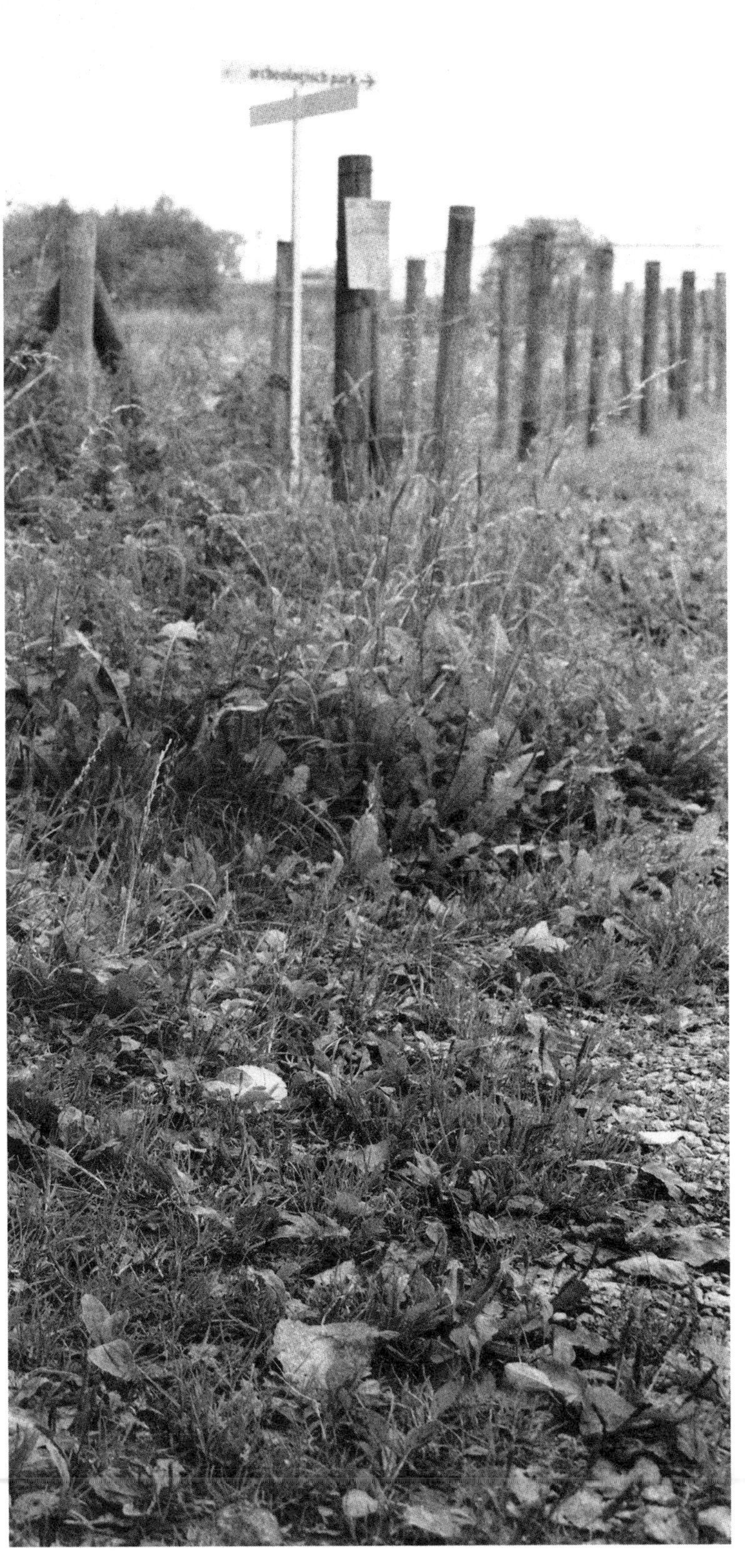

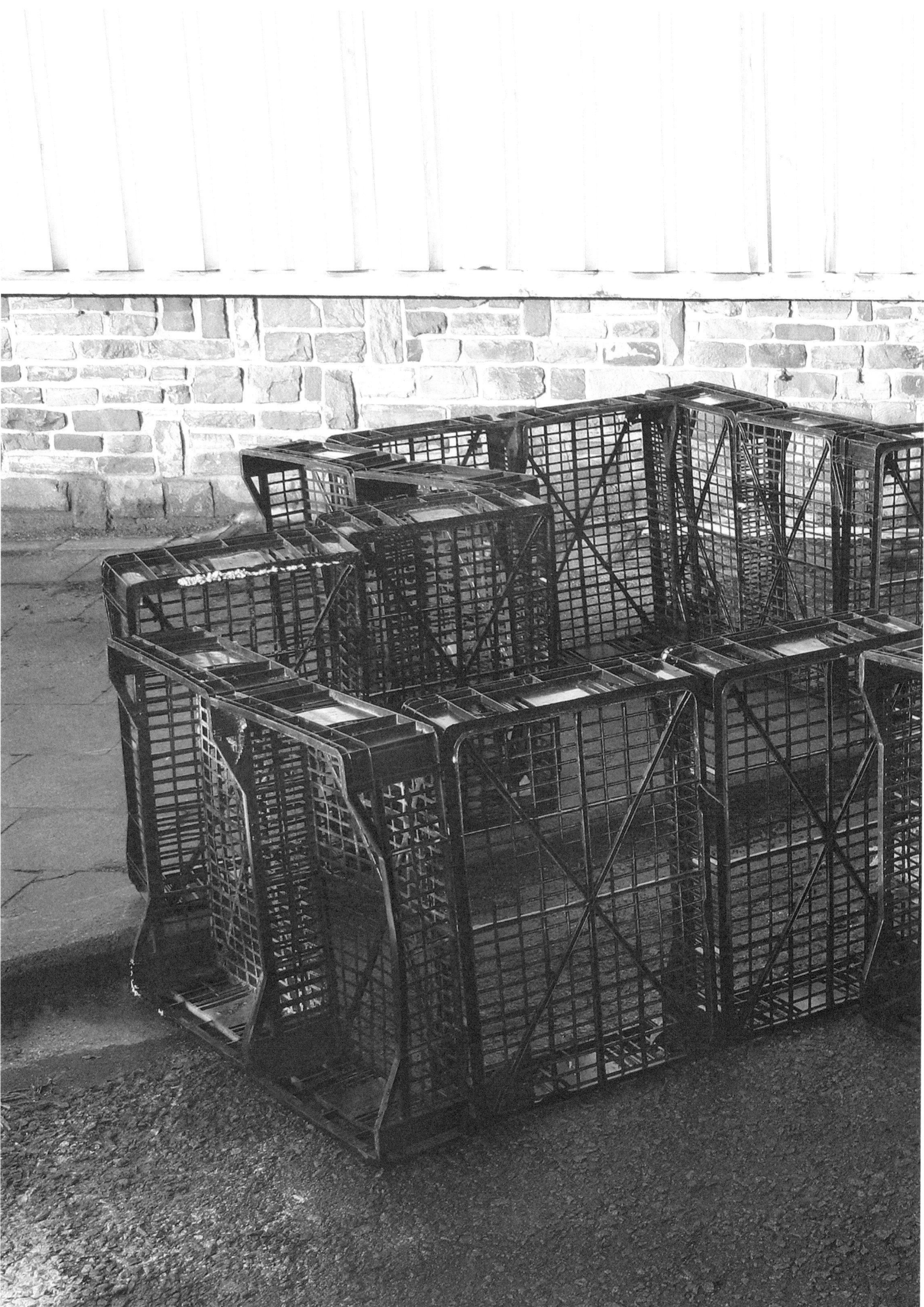

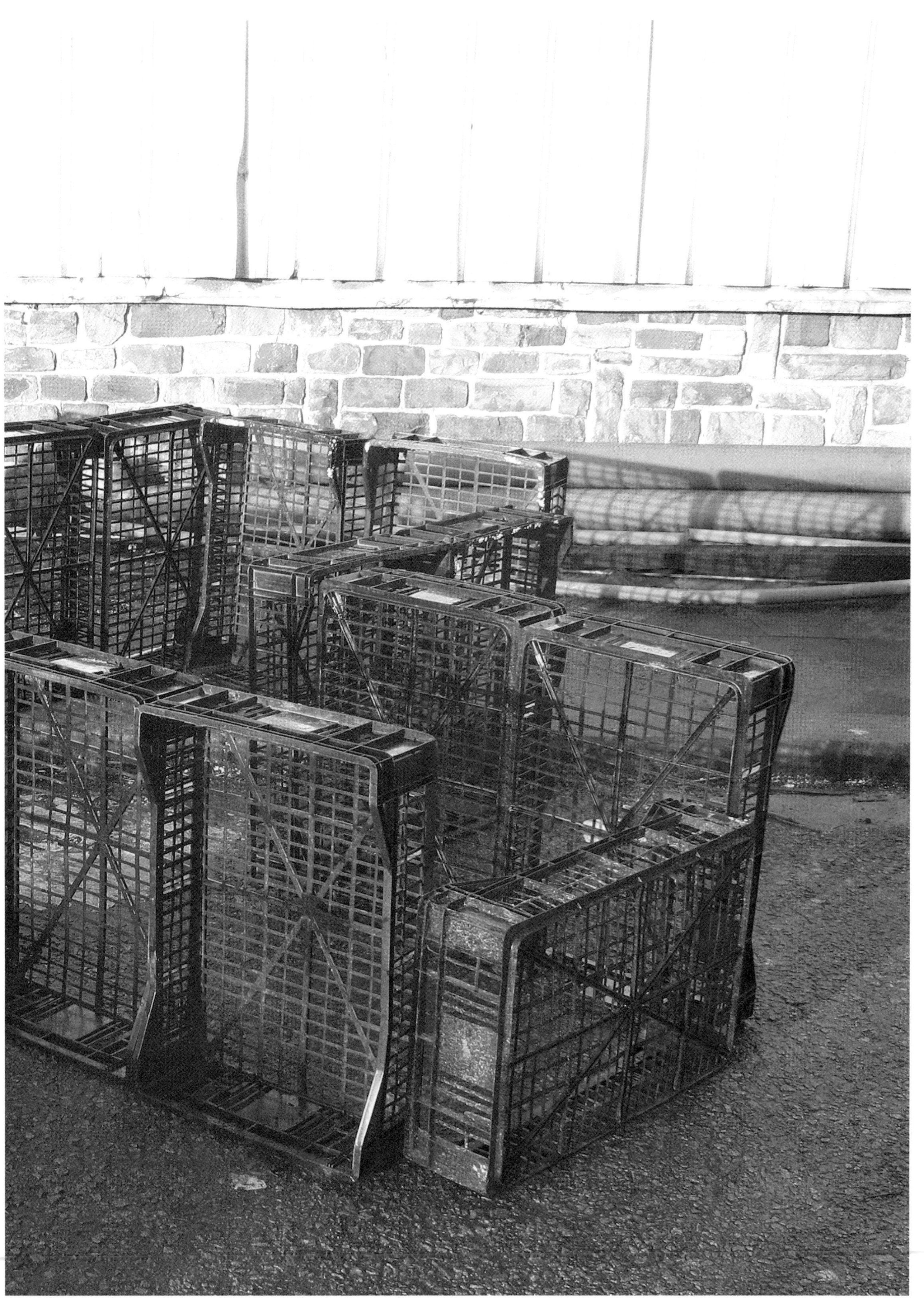

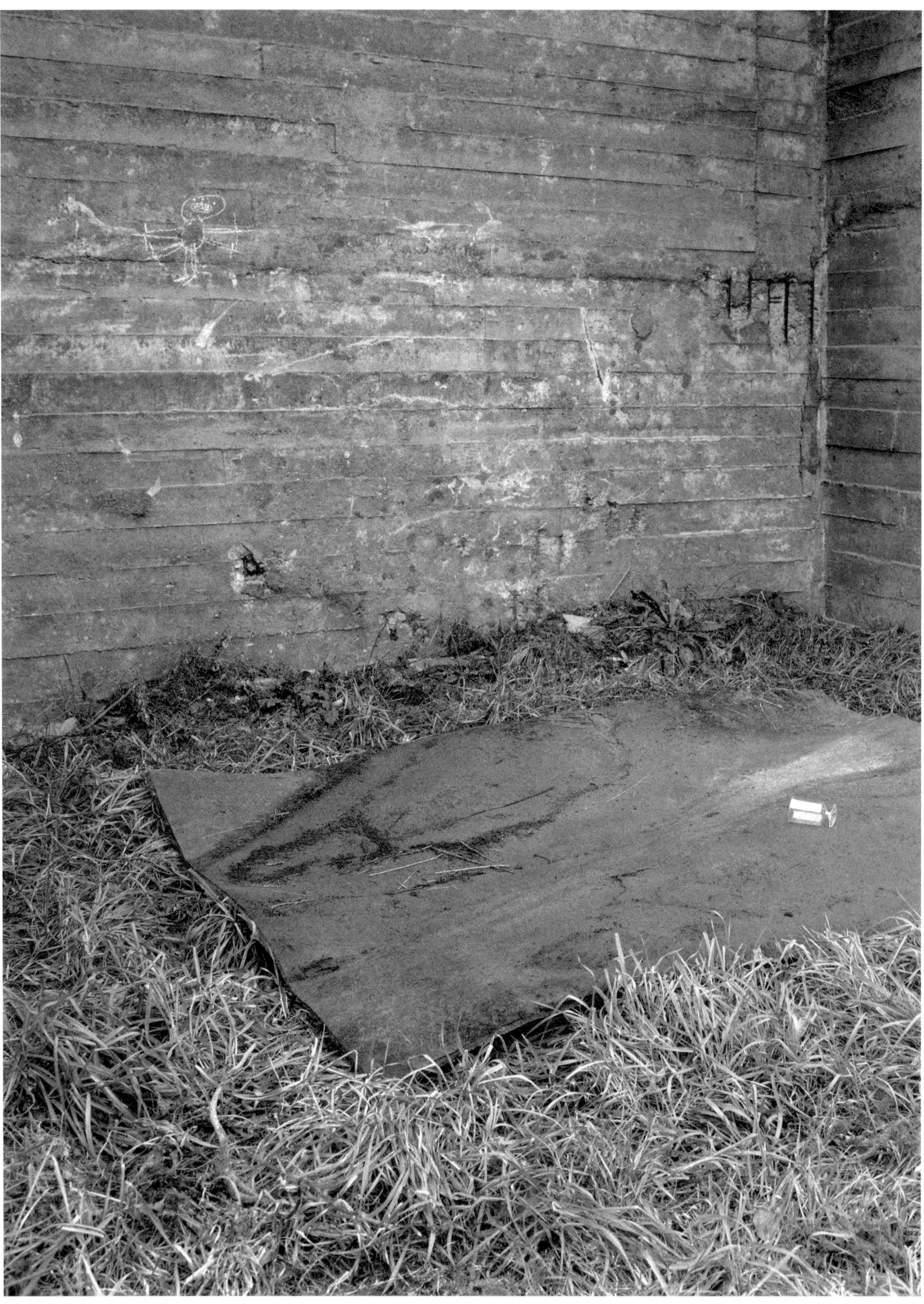

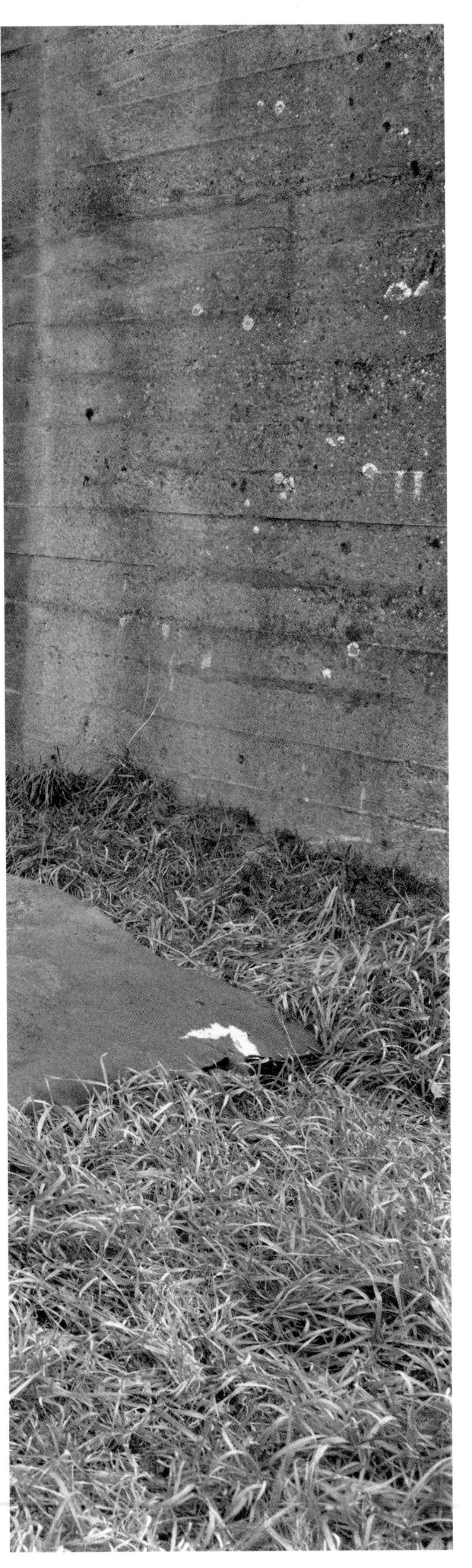

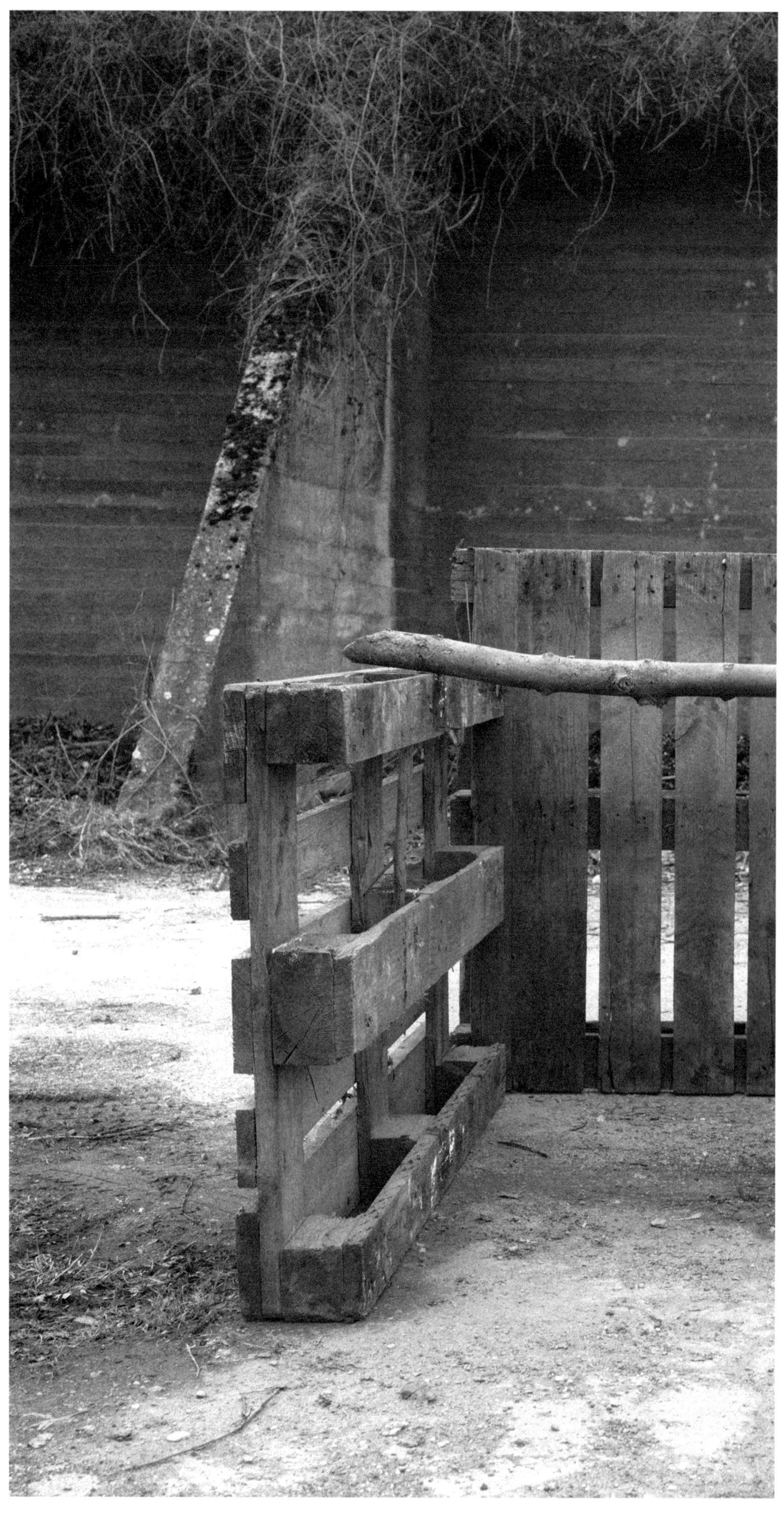

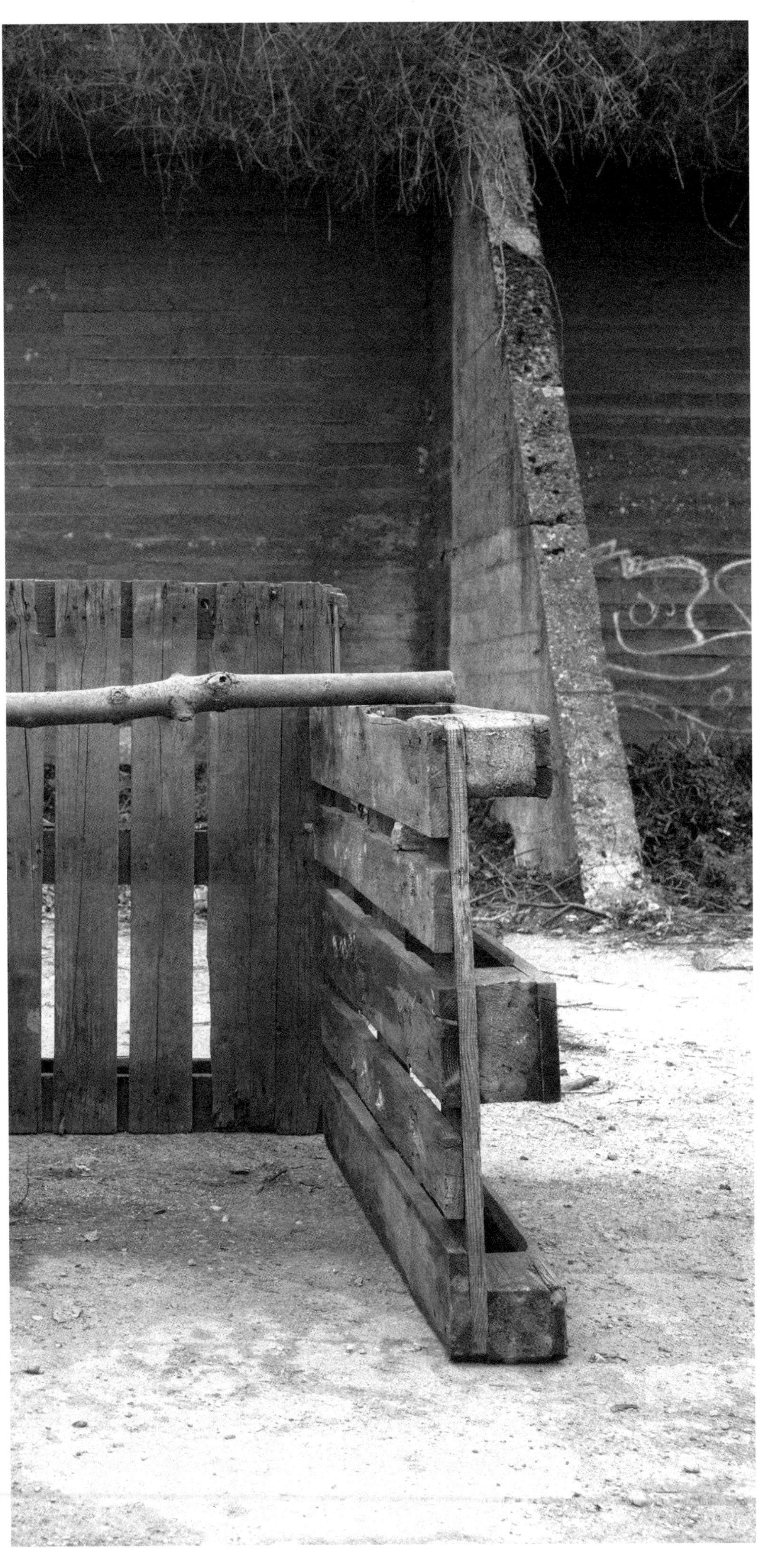

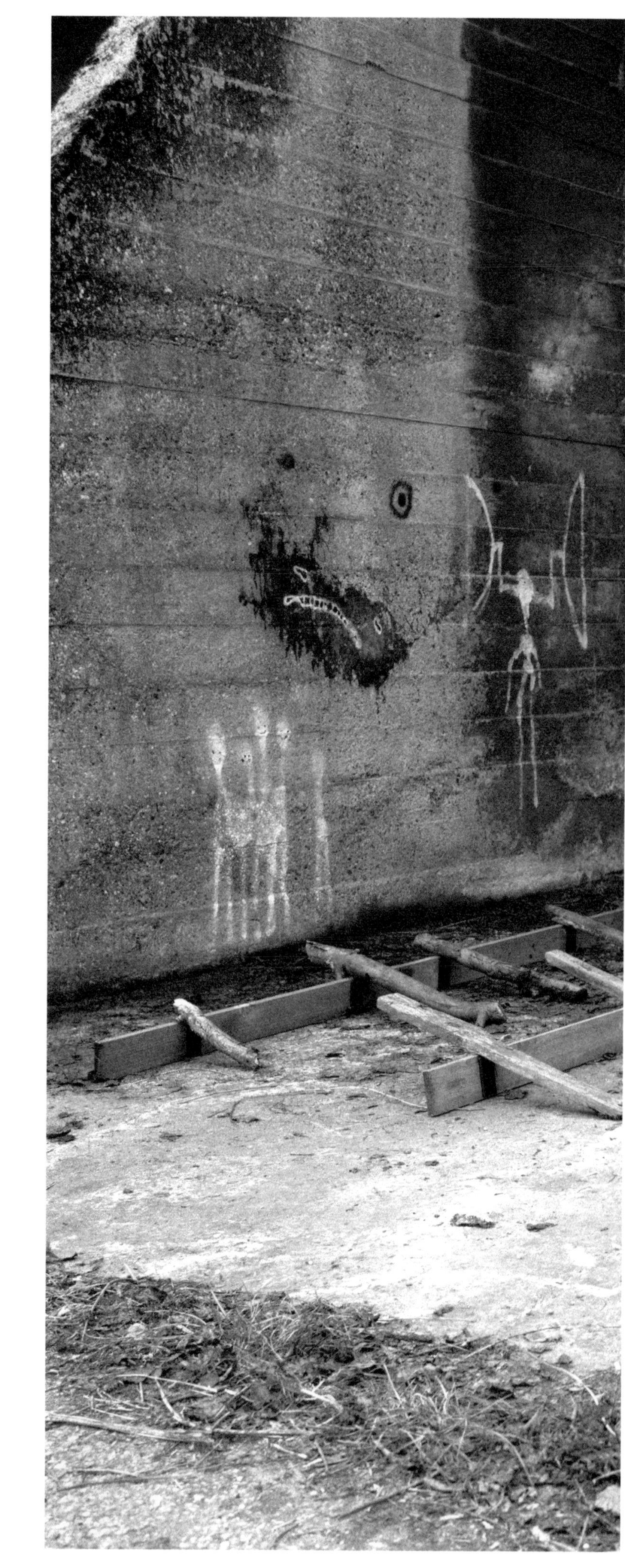

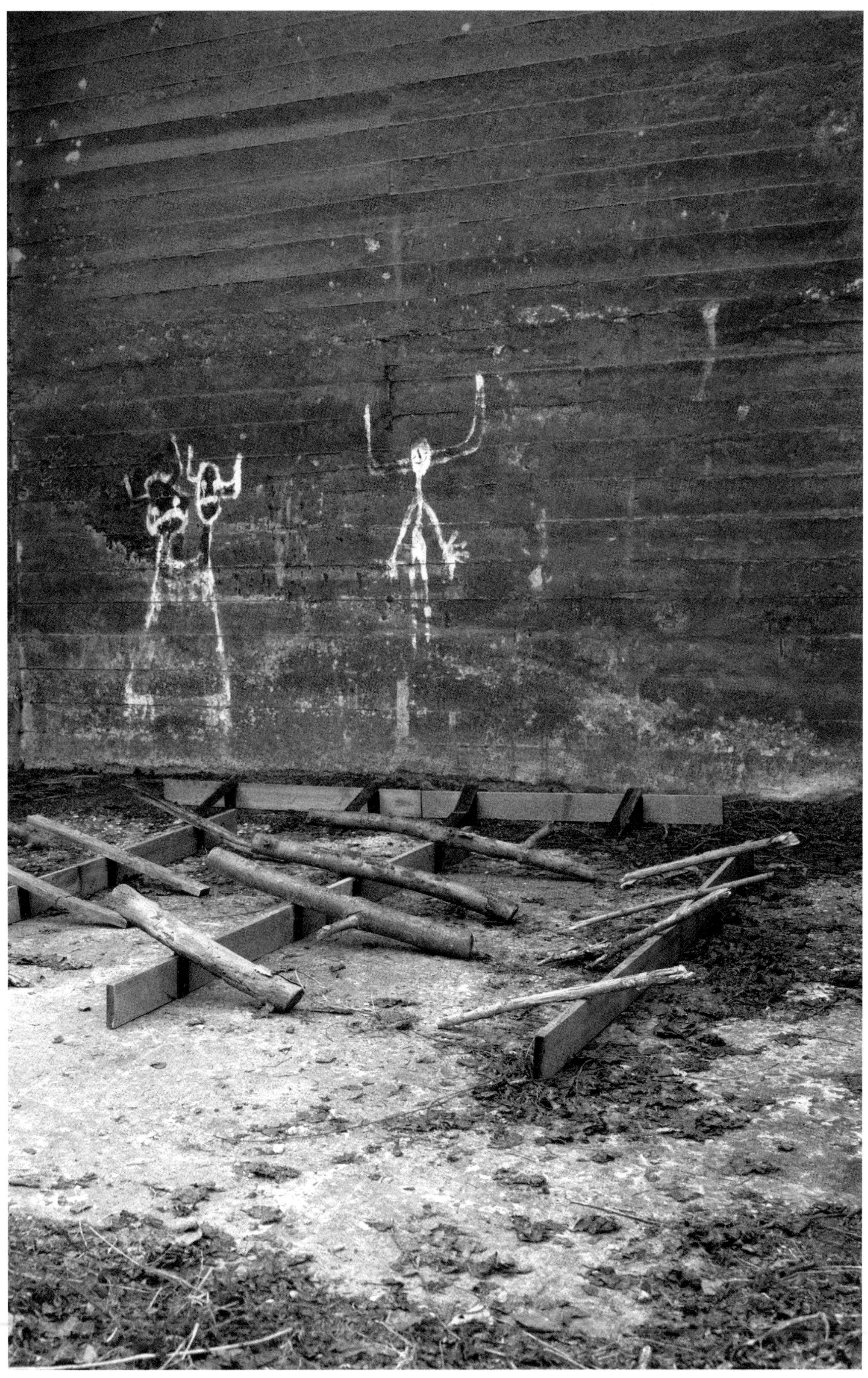

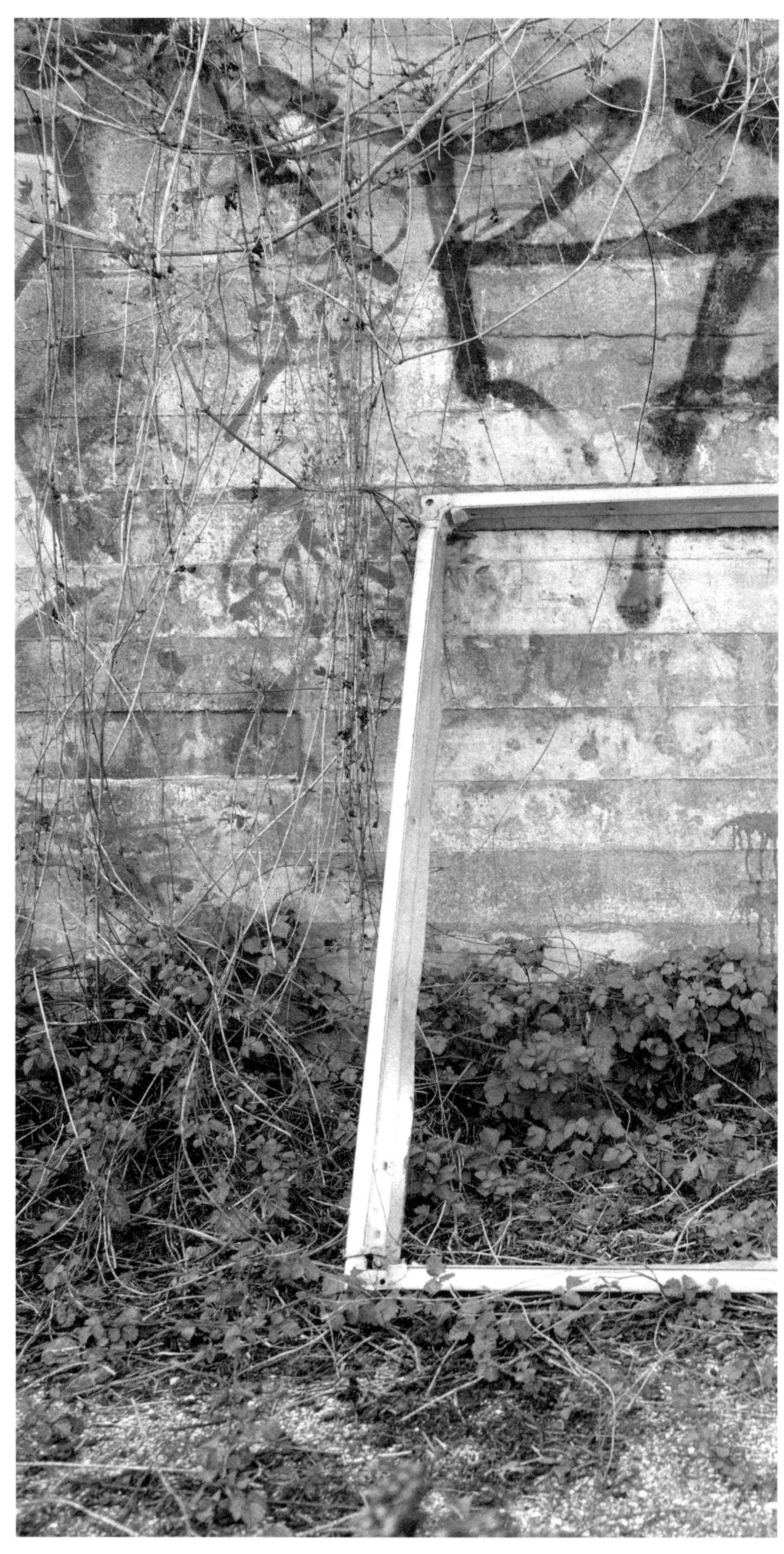

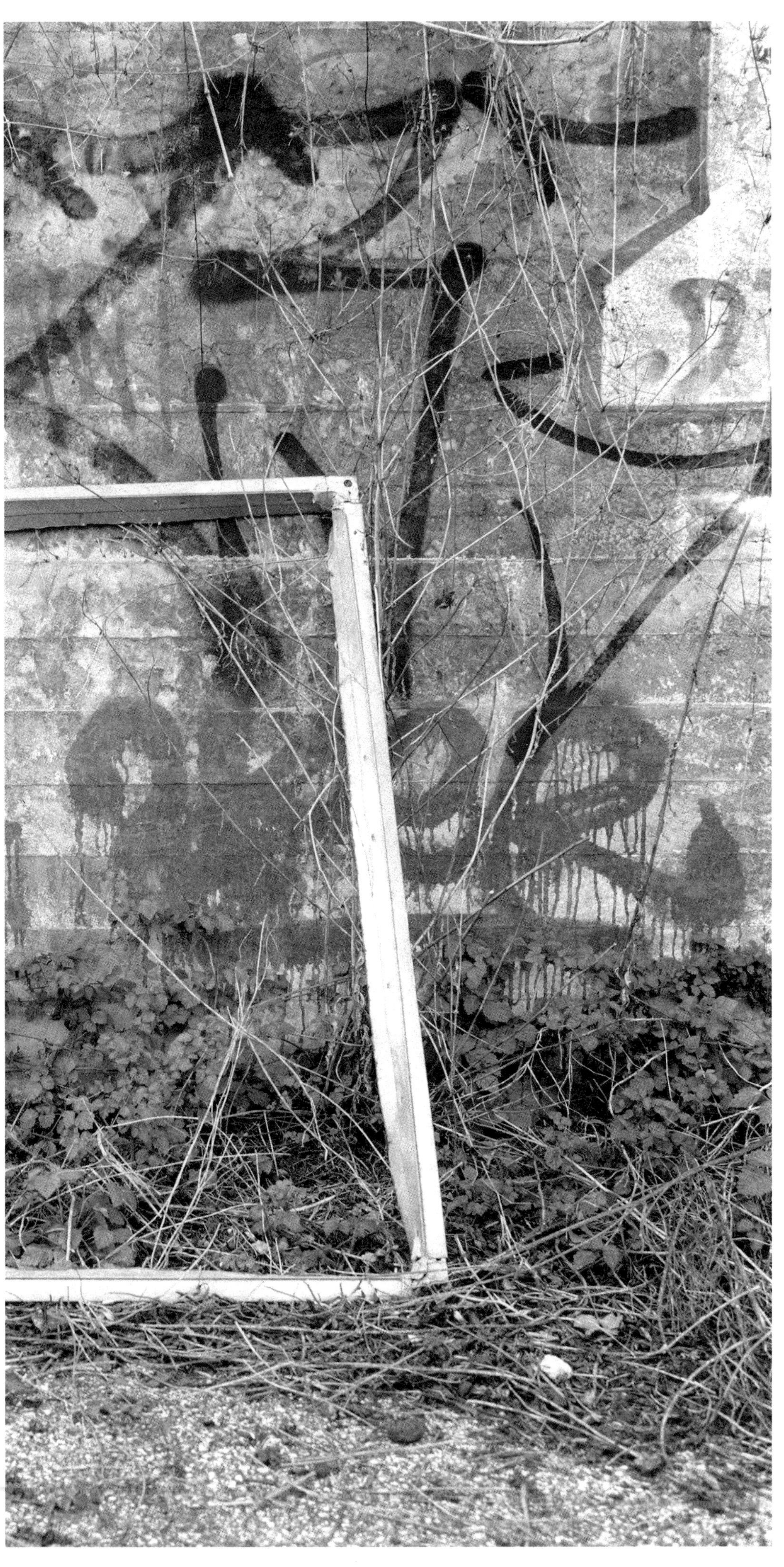

APE#034
Lara Dhondt, WANDERING OFF

ISBN 9789490800185
www.artpapereditions.org
www.laradhondt.be
First edition of 500 copies

Works from the series public sculptures, primary stages and memento (2012-2013).

Lara Dhondt is represented by Bourouina gallery, Berlin.

Graphic design: Studio Jurgen Maelfeyt
Printing: New Goff, Ghent
First print: November 2013